ESSENTIAL
ITALIAN LAKES

Original text by Richard Sale
Revised and updated by Barbara Rogers and Stillman Rogers

© AA Media Limited 2008
First published 2008. Revised 2010

ISBN 978-0-7495-6676-0

Published by AA Publishing, a trading name of AA Media Limited, whose registered office is Fanum House, Basing View, Basingstoke, Hampshire RG21 4EA. Registered number 06112600.

A CIP catalogue record for this book is available from the British Library.

All righ| system | recordi | obtaine | dispose | is publi | are bel | respon | conseq | statuto | author' | publish | things

ieval

ch it
cation
o

on the

ıt

Falkirk Council	
BN	
Askews	
914.52	£5.99

Colour separation by AA Digital Department
Printed and bound in Italy by Printer Trento S.r.l.

A04192
Maps in this title produced from mapping © MAIRDUMONT / Falk Verlag 2010
with reference to mapping © ISTITUTO GEOGRAFICO DE AGOSTINI S.p.A., NOVARA 2009
Transport map © Communicarta Ltd, UK

About this book

Symbols are used to denote the following categories:

➕ map reference to maps on cover

✉ address or location

☎ telephone number

🕐 opening times

✋ admission charge

🍴 restaurant or café on premises or nearby

Ⓠ nearest underground train station

▣ nearest bus/tram route

▣ nearest overground train station

▭ nearest ferry stop

✈ nearest airport

❷ other practical information

ⓘ tourist information office

▶ indicates the page where you will find a fuller description

This book is divided into five sections.

The essence of the Italian Lakes pages 6–19
Introduction; Features; Food and drink; Short break, including the 10 Essentials

Planning pages 20–33
Before you go; Getting there; Getting around; Being there

Best places to see pages 34–55
The unmissable highlights of any visit to the Italian Lakes

Best things to do pages 56–69
Great places to have lunch; stunning views; places to take the children and more

Exploring pages 70–185
The best places to visit around the Italian Lakes, organized by area

Maps
All map references are to the maps on the covers. For example, Lugano has the reference ➕ 4B – indicating the grid square in which it is to be found

Admission prices
Inexpensive (under €4)
Moderate (€4–€7)
Expensive (over €7)

Hotel prices
Prices are per room per night: € budget (under €90); €€ moderate (€90–€150); €€€ expensive to luxury (over €150)

Restaurant prices
Price for a three-course meal per person without drinks: € budget (under €35); €€ moderate (€35–€70); €€€ expensive (over €70)

Contents

BEST THINGS TO DO

56 – 69

EXPLORING...

70 – 185

The essence of...

The Italian Lakes, cradled in the arms of pre-Alpine mountains, are among the world's great travel destinations, and have been since the ancient Romans built summer villas here. European royalty followed, gilding the lakes with a glamour that remains untarnished today. But the lakes are far more than just a pretty face. The artistic treasures and rich history that you expect in Italy are all around, from 5,000-year-old rock carvings to medieval masterpieces to buildings by today's foremost architects. And the Italians have mastered another art, one which visitors can enjoy too – the fine art of living.

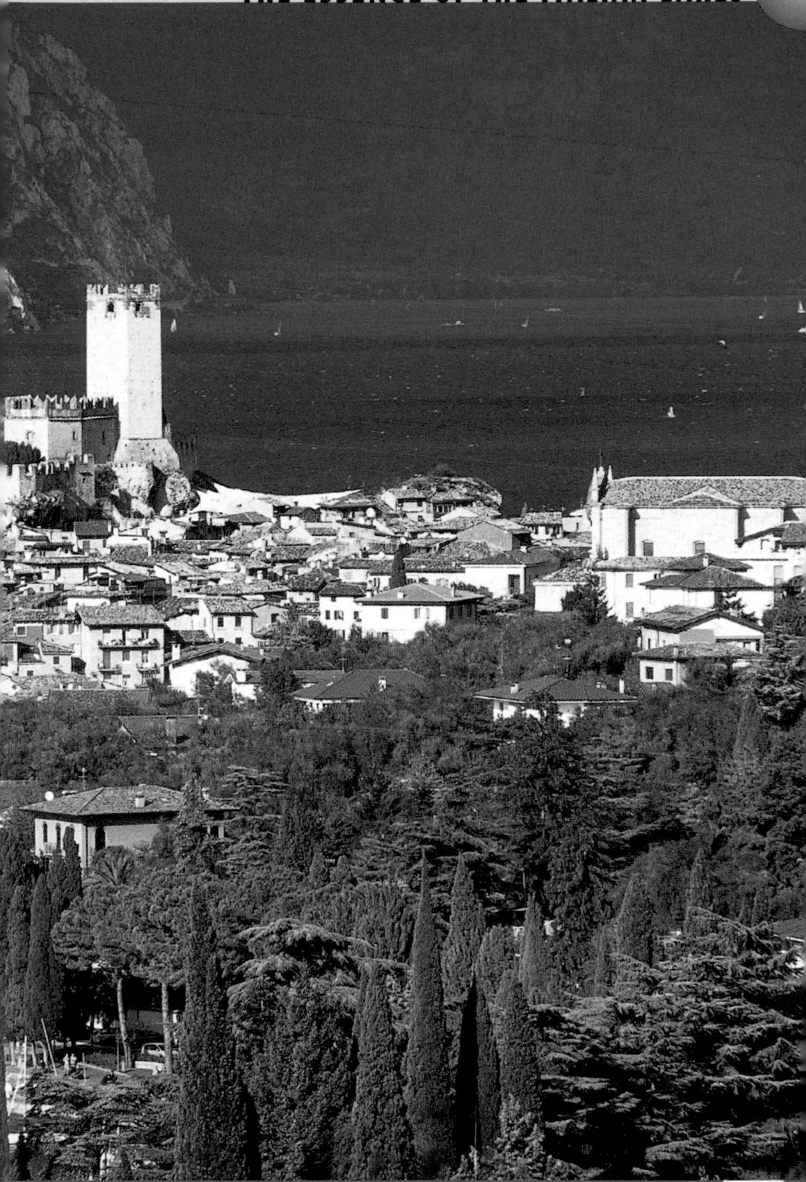

features

The Italian Lakes are superbly situated for the visitor. They are just a short distance from the high peaks that mark the border between Italy and Switzerland; an equally short journey from the great Renaissance cities of the Lombardy Plain – Cremona and Mantua; and within reach of Venice, one of the world's most fascinating cities. From lakes Maggiore and Como it is just an hour or so south to the treasures of Milan; from southern Lake Garda it takes even less time to reach historic Verona. Between the two are Bréscia, with some of the best Roman ruins in Italy, and Bergamo, an almost complete, virtually traffic-free, walled Renaissance town. North of Lake Garda lie the spiky towers of the Brenta Dolomites.

Focusing on these nearby places, however, it is easy to ignore the lakes themselves. The enviable climate (warm summers and crisp winters) and natural beauty of the area have attracted visitors for centuries. Rich and artistic Romans built villas here, a tradition that was revived in the 19th century – a string of villas, from the sumptuous to the simple, were built along the shores. The combination of water, sunshine and the fertile soil surrounding the lakes allowed the villa builders to cultivate magnificent gardens.

Despite the fact that the lakes share these advantages, they are each quite different in character. Orta, hemmed in by high ridges, is secretive; Maggiore busy, yet peaceful. Lugano is very Swiss, while Como is very beautiful and elegant. The eastern lakes, Iseo and Garda, are the holiday lakes, Garda especially – the beaches of its eastern shore are enjoyed by sun worshippers. Add food at its Italian best, wines from the Franciacorta and Garda's shore, and lake steamers that take the strain out of local excursions, and the Italian Lakes offer the perfect holiday destination.

LAKE MAGGIORE
- Despite the name, Maggiore is not the biggest of the lakes but it is the longest. From Magadino, in Switzerland, to Sesto Calende is 65km (40 miles).
- The lake covers 215sq km (84sq miles).
- At its deepest point it is 372m (1,220ft) deep.
- About 15 per cent of the lake lies in Switzerland.

LAKE LUGANO
- The lake is 36km (22.5 miles) long, but very narrow, rarely more than 2km (1.25 miles) wide.
- The maximum depth of the lake is 288m (945ft).
- The causeway that carries the road and railway across the lake cuts it into two separate areas.
- About 60 per cent of the lake lies in Switzerland.

LAKE COMO
- Lake Como is the deepest of the lakes. The deepest point, which lies off the shore of Argegno, is 414m (1,358ft).
- The lake has an area of 148sq km (58sq miles).
- Because of its shape, the lake's shoreline measures 170km (105 miles).
- Although the lake has two arms, only one of them – the Lecco arm – has an outflowing river.

LAKE GARDA
- Lake Garda, the largest lake, covers 370sq km (144sq miles). The lake has a maximum depth of 346m (1,135ft).
- Despite its size, the lake's shoreline measures only 125km (77 miles).
- Garda is the only lake without a significant island, though it does have a handful of tiny islets.

MILAN
- With a population of about 1.3 million, Milan is Italy's second-biggest city after Rome.

food & drink

The lakes area serves a typically northern-Italian menu, though there are a few local specialities. As with everywhere in Italy, the meal will consist of generous helpings and be served with a smile. In addition, the restaurant is likely to have a terrace overlooking the water. As a result, there will be three delights to every meal – the food, the service and the setting.

RISTORANTE, TRATTORIA OR PIZZERIA?

Of these, the pizzeria is the cheapest and quickest eating house. The menu usually consists of pizzas only, although some also serve a limited range of pasta dishes and may even have a grill. Trattorias serve a more extensive menu, but the meals will be straightforward, with minimum frills. The *ristorante* can vary from somewhere serving a limited range of meals, but of the highest quality – a fish restaurant for example – to one serving a very wide range. The majority of Italian restaurants serve excellent meals from kitchens of the highest standard. But here, as everywhere, menus can vary from the simple to the very highest standard of

international cuisine, with meals from the plain and simple to the adventurous and elaborate.

FOOD

Pasta is a mainstay, of course, but there is also a surprising amount of rice eaten. To the south of Milan, around Pavia, there are extensive rice fields – a fact that surprises many visitors – and rice dishes are a speciality. *Risotto alla Milanese*, a hearty rice dish made with saffron, is found all over the lakes area. Rice is also often served with fish. The lakes are home to many species of fish but which is best is, of course, a matter of opinion. Try the perch, which is exquisite, or lake trout, the other favourite. For something very different, try *missoltini,* sun-dried fish.

Meals can begin with small portions of pasta or rice, but minestrone soup is often on the menu. Made with fresh local vegetables, it can be a meal on its own. Meat dishes tend to be veal or steak, though lamb *(agnello)* and various game meats, such as boar *(cinghiale)* can also be found. The famed meat speciality is *osso bucco*, veal braised with white wine and onions. Another speciality, not often found on menus, is *polpette*, meatballs stuffed with parmesan and ricotta. Around Lake Orta the speciality is *asino* – donkey, usually stewed leg – while in the nearby Ossola valley they favour *viulin* – salted leg of goat. On the mountains around Lake Como, rabbit *(coniglio)* is popular, while the Valtellina (the valley from north Como to Sondrio) produces *bresaola* – dried salt beef. Rabbit is also a favourite meat in Bergamo cooking, where it is usually preceded by local pastas such as ravioli with sage and butter. Many meat dishes will be served with *funghi* (mushrooms). Try the porcini, which have a distinctive, mellow flavour.

Vegetarians will be able to enjoy the minestrone, one of the highlights of Italian cooking, and pasta dishes such as vegetable lasagne and spinach *panzerotti*. There are also delicious vegetable dishes such as aubergines (eggplants) baked in cheese. Vegans will need to ensure that their chosen pasta is egg-free. There are several very good vegetarian restaurants in Milan.

DRINK

Northern Italy is known among connoisseurs for its fine wines – Barolo, Barbaresco and Barbera from the Piemonte, Amarone from Valpolicella and the premium whites of the Franciacorta. Less well-known, but thoroughly enjoyable, are reds from Bardolino on Lake Garda. The Ticino – the region of Switzerland that surrounds Lake Lugano and northern Maggiore – produces excellent wines so treasured locally that they rarely make it to world markets. Labels will designate a wine's origin – DS (Denominazione Semplice) has no quality standard; DOC (Denominazione di Origine Controllata) wines meet defined standards and come from officially recognized regions; while DCG (Denominazione

Controllata e Garanzia) are wines of the highest standard. Don't hesitate to ask for a taste *(prova)* of the local house wine *(vino de tavola)*. These are often quite good and you may discover some local treasure that never makes it beyond the village where you drink it.

DEFINITELY NOT WIENERSCHNITZEL

One of the standards on most local menus is *Cotoletta alla Milanese*, breaded veal cutlets. In view of the former Austrian domination of the area, visitors are advised not to refer to this course as Wienerschnitzel, even if the observation is accurate enough.

TO STAND OR SIT

In cafés and bars you often pay for your drink first, presenting the payment slip with your order to the man behind the bar who makes the drink. In many places, a higher price is charged for sitting with your coffee than for standing with it at the bar. If you go for the latter, ask the cashier for your drink *al banco* (at the counter).

ASK THE LOCALS

Wherever you go, look for local specialities. A good place to start is at *pasticcerie*, pastry shops that nearly always have café tables. Around Lake Garda, look for *Torta delle Rose*, a delicious cake made with rosewater. In the Swiss towns, look for red polenta, ground from a heritage maize variety known only here. Ask to sample local cheeses. Some, such as Taleggio, are well-known worldwide, while others may be unknown outside their local valley.

short break

If you only have a short time to visit the Italian Lakes, or would like to get a really complete picture of the area, here are the essentials:

● **Take a boat ride.** With all that water it would be a crime not to, but there are other advantages – some lakeside villas and villages look best from the water.

● **Go uphill to view the lake.** Lake views from the shores are splendid, but to see the lakes at their best it is necessary to climb to one of the retaining ridges.

● **Go shopping.** It may sound like a cliché, but for leather Italy has few equals and for silk Como is the place. And then there are the fashion houses of Milan…

- **Eat alfresco.** With the perfect climate and lake views how could anyone not?

- **Buy an ice cream.** All towns and most villages have shops selling ice creams and sorbets in the wonderful tastes of local sun-ripened fruits.

- **Go for a walk.** Not only do the high ridges above the lakes offer superb views, they are a paradise for the flower lover.

- **Learn to windsurf.** The lakes have some of the most dependable winds in Europe. The air is warm even if the water is cool, and there is no chance of being blown miles out to sea.

- **Visit a villa or garden.** One of the great features of the lakes is their villas and gardens, and no visit would be complete without visiting at least one.

- **Take a stroll.** Italians share with the Spanish the habit of an evening stroll – to meet friends or just to be seen.

- **Visit a city.** While on holiday you might be tempted to avoid the hustle and bustle of a city. Italian cities are different, however, as they are virtually open-air museums. Bergamo, Verona, Brescia and central Milan are all very fine and are close to the lakes.

Planning

Before you go

WHEN TO GO

JAN	FEB	MAR	APR	MAY	JUN	JUL	AUG	SEP	OCT	NOV	DEC
6°C	7°C	10°C	13°C	18°C	21°C	24°C	23°C	18°C	12°C	10°C	8°C
43°F	45°F	50°F	55°F	64°F	70°F	75°F	73°F	64°F	55°F	50°F	46°F

🌧️ High season 🌧️ Low season

There is no bad time to visit the Italian Lakes. In spring the flowers are a delight while in summer the sun shines all day every day, or so it seems, with the cool waters of the lakes offering a chance to escape the occasionally very hot midday hours. By autumn the very hot days of summer have been replaced by a gentler warmth. Then winter brings snow to the high ridges, though at the lakeside severe cold is a rarity.

WHAT YOU NEED

● Required
○ Suggested
▲ Not required

Some countries require a passport to remain valid for a minimum period (usually at least six months) beyond the date of entry – contact their consulate or embassy or your travel agency for details.

	UK	Germany	USA	Netherlands	Spain
Passport	●	●	●	●	●
Visa (regulations can change – check before making reservations)	▲	▲	▲	▲	▲
Onward or return ticket	▲	▲	▲	▲	▲
Health inoculations	▲	▲	▲	▲	▲
Health documentation (➤ 23, Health Insurance)	●	●	●	●	●
Travel insurance	○	○	○	○	○
Driving licence (national)	●	●	●	●	●
Car insurance certificate (if own car)	●	●	●	●	●
Car registration document (if own car)	●	●	●	●	●

WEBSITES

● Lake Orta and west Lake Maggiore: www.distrettolaghi.it
● Lake Como: www.lakecomo.com
● Milan: http://turismo.provincia.milano.it

- Varese and east Lake Maggiore:
  www.vareselandoftourism.it
- North Lake Maggiore:
  www.maggiore.ch
- Lake Lugano:
  www.lugano-tourism.ch
- Bergamo:
  http://turismo.provincia.bergamo.it
- Bréscia and west Lake Garda:
  www.provincia.brescia.it
- Verona and east Lake Garda:
  www.tourism.verona.it
- North Lake Garda:
  www.visittrentino.it

TOURIST OFFICES AT HOME

In the UK
Italian State Tourist Board (ENIT)
Offices, 1 Princes Street
London, W1R 8AY
☎ 020 7408 1254

In the USA
USA Suite 1565,
Rockefeller Center,

630 Fifth Avenue
New York, NY 10111
☎ 212/245-5618

Suite 550
12400 Wilshire Boulevard
Los Angeles
CA 90025
☎ 310/820-1898

HEALTH INSURANCE

EU nationals can get free or reduced-rate emergency medical treatment with the relevant documentation (European Health Insurance Card – EHIC – for UK nationals) although private medical insurance is strongly recommended and is essential for all other visitors.

The EHIC also covers emergency dentistry. Visitors with their own dental health insurance should obtain advice from their insurers.

TIME DIFFERENCES

| GMT | Italy | Germany | USA (NY) | Netherlands | Spain |
| 12 noon | 1PM | 1PM | 7AM | 1PM | 1PM |

Italy is one hour ahead of Greenwich Mean Time (GMT+1), but from late March to late September daylight saving time (GMT+2) operates.

NATIONAL HOLIDAYS

1 January *New Year's Day*

6 January *Epiphany*

Mar/Apr *Easter Sunday and Monday*

25 April *Liberation Day*

1 May *Labour Day*

2 June *National Day*

15 August *Assumption Day*

1 November *All Saints' Day*

8 December *Immaculate Conception*

25 and 26 December *Christmas*

WHAT'S ON WHEN

1–6 January *Christmas cribs* (crèche scenes), called *presepi*, are displayed in Bardolino, Peschiera, Torri del Benaco and at the Arena in Verona (www.gardainforma.com).

February *Carnival season.* The most famous carnival is at Venice. Within the lakes area, the best is the *Gnoccho Bacchanalia*, at Verona. Milan celebrates with parades in the streets around Piazza Duomo.

March *Milano Moda Donna*: Women's Fashion Week for autumn styles (www.cameramoda.com).

Easter *Processions* in the Swiss villages of Lake Lugano, often held on both Maundy Thursday and Good Friday.

Late June *Festival of Ancient Music* is held in Orta San Giúlio.

c24 June Sunday after St John the Baptist's Day, boats process to Isola Comacina, Lake Como, for Mass in the ruined church.

June–July *Shakespeare season*, Verona.

July *Folklore Festival*, Val Cannobina, Lake Maggiore.
Festival of traditional music and dance, at Quarna Sopra, Lake Orta.
Jazz Festival, Lugano (first week of the month).
Music Festival, Lugano (last week of the month).
International Sailing Regatta, Gargagno, Lake Garda.

July–August *Opera season*, Verona, staged open-air in the Roman Arena (www.arena.it).
Season of open-air plays at Il Vittoriale, Gardone Riviera, Lake Garda (www.vittoriale.it).

Mid-August to mid-September *International Music Festival (Settimane Musicali)*, Stresa, Lake Maggiore. World-famous event with top musicians and conductors.
Lake Como Festival brings music to various lakeside venues (www.lakecomofestival.com).

September *Firework Spectacular*, Sirmione, Lake Garda.
Windsurf Festival in Torbole.

September to mid-October *Music Festival*, Ascona, Lake Maggiore, timed so that some of the players from Stresa can appear again.

Mid-September to October Lake Maggiore villages celebrate festivals of local foods with special menus in the restaurants.

September or October *Grape Festival*, Bardolino, Lake Garda (last weekend of September or first weekend of October).

October *Milano Moda Donna:* women's spring styles hit the catwalks (www.cameramoda.com).

December *First night of the opera season*, Milan (7 December; www.teatroallascala.org).
Several towns on Lake Garda display life-sized Christmas nativity scenes.

Getting there

BY AIR

International flights Milan's Linate airport, to the east of the city, is notorious for being fog-bound. That was one reason why a new airport, Malpensa, was built at Somma Lombardo, close to the southern tip of Lake Maggiore. Plans to use Linate for domestic flights only have not come to fruition, although the majority of international flights do land at Malpensa. Malpensa is close to the A26 *autostrada,* which makes its way to the west of Lake Maggiore, at present ending west of Stresa. To the south the A26 links to the A4, offering a quick way to the other lakes. Linate sits on the Milan *autostrada* ring road, but visitors returning to it for the flight home should note that if travelling south on the ring road the Linate exit is from the left lane (the fast lane) not from the right lane as would be expected. For those not renting a car, both Malpensa and Linate have bus connections to Milan, from where trains depart for both sides of Lake Maggiore, but only Como on Lake Como and Desenzano del Garda on Lake Garda.

Some UK low-cost carriers do use Malpensa. They also use Orio al Serio, which sits on the A4 south of Bergamo. This is extremely convenient for all the lakes. Low-cost carriers also use Treviso, east of Lake Garda. This is more convenient for Venice than the lakes, but may be useful to some travellers. Linate is about 20 minutes from Milan, Malpensa is about an hour by bus and about 35 minutes by train. Train and bus times to the major lake resorts from Milan are:

Como	Train 1 hour	Bus 1.5 hours
Stresa	Train 1 hour	Bus 1.5 hours
Desenzano	Train 1 hour	Bus 1 hour

Useful contact details and flight information from:
Linate and Malpensa ☎ 02 7485 2200; www.sea-aeroportimilano.it
Orio al Serio ☎ 035 326 323; www.orioaeroporto.it

Domestic flights Italy's domestic air service is operated by Alitalia. Reserve ahead as planes are crowded in the summer season. Full-time students under 26 receive a 25 per cent discount on internal flight fares. For airport information at Malpensa or Linate ☎ 02 74852200. In addition to Malpensa, Linate and Orio al Serio airports, there is an airport at Verona (Villafranca).

BY TRAIN

Milan is accessible from most major mainland European capitals, including Paris, through which there are connections to the UK. Trains from Milan reach destinations on the eastern side of Lake Orta. On Lake Maggiore trains run along the western shore as far north as Baveno, and along the eastern shore to Switzerland. Como city is easily reached by train, as is the eastern shore of Lake Como, north from Lecco. However, train links to the western shore are poor. Lake Iseo's eastern shore is also accessible by train, but on Lake Garda, only Desenzano and Peschiera have train stations.

The motorail services linking Boulogne and Paris with Milan's Porta Garibaldi station have been cancelled.

Several of the rail routes across the Alps are highly scenic, and well worth travelling by daylight. Although most tunnel through the highest reaches, they still travel through spectacular landscapes on the way. Particularly interesting is the route from Zurich, Switzerland, to Milan, which loops three times through the corkscrew St Gottard Tunnel.

BY ROAD

There are long-distance bus services from mainland European capitals to Milan, although many routes may not be direct and can therefore be slow. Drivers can reach Lake Maggiore by way of the Aosta Valley from France or the Simplon Pass from Switzerland. Lakes Lugano and Como are also accessible from Switzerland. Lake Garda is best approached over the Brenner Pass from Austria.

The A4 *autostrada* links Turin and Venice, passing close to Milan (the city ring road links with it), Bergamo, Bréscia and the southern tip of Lake Garda. The A8 links the A4 to Varese. The A26 leaves the A8 close to Gallarate (and Malpensa airport) and is handy for getting to Lake Orta and southwestern Lake Maggiore. The A9 links the A4 to Como city, continuing into Switzerland to reach Lake Lugano. The A12 links the A4 to the Brenner Pass and is excellent for those driving to Riva del Garda as the lakeside roads can be congested in summer.

Getting around

PUBLIC TRANSPORT

Trains Italy has a good rail system. A 'Travel at Will' pass is available for 8, 15, 21 or 30 days and offers unlimited travel on any train. Reduced-rate passes are available for visitors under 26 and senior citizens. Italy has various classes of train: *Super-Rapido/TEE* offer first-class-only travel, running between the major cities; a supplement is charged and seats must be booked. *Rapido* (fast) trains offer different levels of service and seats do not have to be reserved. *Espresso* (long-distance) are express trains with limited stops. *Diretto* provide a slower service stopping at most stations, while *Locale* stop at all stations. In addition to the main system, there are a few private lines. Two of these link Como and Laveno to Milan.

Buses Passengers on city buses must buy a ticket from bars or machines before starting their journey and must validate it on the bus by inserting it into a machine that overprints the date and time. The ticket allows unlimited travel for usually one hour.

Ferries All the lakes have steamer services. Boat passes are available for one day, several days, or one or two weeks. Hydrofoils *(aliscafi)* are fast, but do not stop at all villages. The slower boats stop more often but even these boats do not always stop at every village.

TAXIS

Taxis are available at all airports, railway and bus stations and at certain places within large towns and cities. You can't usually hail a passing taxi, but restaurants or hotels will call for one for you.

FARES AND TICKETS

Train tickets are available single *(andata)* or return *(andata e ritorno)*. The trains have first and second classes. Tickets for journeys of up to 250km

(155 miles) can be bought from newspaper kiosks and tobacconists at the station and must be validated by entering them into the time-punch machine on the train. For longer journeys tickets must be bought at the ticket counter and will be valid for the day of travel. A *Carta Verde* offers a 20 per cent discount to those aged 12–26, while a *Carta d'Argento* offers the same discount to over 60s. Non-residents below the age of 26 can obtain a *Trenitalia Pass*, which allows unlimited travel during a 2-month period. The Pass is not valid over the Christmas period or at certain other times.

Tickets for the Milan metro can be bought at station counters, kiosks or at automatic ticket machines. As for shorter train journeys and buses, the ticket must be validated at the machine on board.

DRIVING

- Speed limits on motorways: 130kph (80mph)
- When the road is wet all traffic is restricted to 110kph (68mph).
- Speed limit on dual carriageways: 110kph (68mph); on other roads: 90kph (56mph)
- Speed limit in urban areas: 50kph (31mph)
- Seatbelts are obligatory for drivers and all passengers over the age of seven. Children under 12 years must travel in rear seats and be restrained with an appropriate harness.
- Random breath-testing. Never drive under the influence of alcohol.
- Fuel stations keep shop hours (but may be open later in the evening). Motorway fuel stations also close at night. Very few fuel stations take credit cards, except on the *autostradas*.
- A red warning triangle must be carried and used at a breakdown or accident. Police speedtrap detectors are illegal. Low-beam headlights are compulsory in tunnels. To drive on Swiss motorways you must display a vignette, a tax disc valid for one year, available at border crossings and fuel stations.
- The Touring Club of Italy (TCI) offers a breakdown service ☎ 116. If your car is hired, follow the hirer's instructions.

CAR RENTAL

All the major car-rental companies are represented at Italian airports and railway stations and in the major towns and cities.

Being there

TOURIST OFFICES
Lake Maggiore
Corso Italia 18, 28838 Stresa
☎ 0323 30416
www.illagomaggiore.com

Lake Como
Piazza Cavour 17, 22100 Como
☎ 031 269712
www.lakecomo.it

Lake Garda
Corso Repubblica 8
25083 Gardone Riviera
☎ 0365 20347

Porto Vecchio 34
25015 Desenzano del Garda
☎ 030 9141510
www.visitgarda.com

Milan
Via Marconi 1
20123 Milano
☎ 02 725241
www.visitamilano.it/turismo_en

Bréscia
Piazza della Loggia 13
25121 Bréscia
☎ 030 2400357;
www.comune.brescia.it

Verona
Via degli Alpini 9 (beside Palazzo
Municipale, Piazza Bra)
37100 Verona
☎ 045 806 8680
www.tourism.verona.it

MONEY
The euro (€) is the official currency of Italy. Notes are issued in
denominations of 5, 10, 20, 50, 100, 200 and 500 euros; coins in
denominations of 1, 2, 5, 10, 20 and 50 cents, and 1 and 2 euros.
Traveller's cheques are accepted by most hotels and a few shops and
restaurants, but the rate of exchange may be less favourable than in
banks. Banks are found in all towns and most villages. ATMs are common.

TIPS/GRATUITIES

Yes ✓ No ✗		
Restaurants (10% usually included)	✓	10%
Cafés/bars (if service not included)	✓	change
Taxis (10% usually included)	✓	10%
Chambermaids/porters	✓	€1–2

POSTAL AND INTERNET SERVICES

Post offices are usually open Monday–Friday 8/8:30–1, 3–6, Saturday 9–12. With the increase in home internet access, internet cafés have become scarce, even in cities, but more hotels now offer internet access. For more information, ask at tourist offices.

TELEPHONES

Most public telephones take cards. Phone cards for €2.50, €5 or €15 can be bought from tobacconists, bars and post offices. Some telephones take coins of 10, 20 or 50 cents or €1 or €2.

International dialling codes
From Italy to:
UK: 00 44
Germany: 00 49
Switzerland: 00 41
USA: 00 1

Emergency phone numbers
Police: 113
Fire: 115
Ambulance: 118

EMBASSIES AND CONSULATES

UK ☎ 02 723001
Germany ☎ 02 6231101

USA ☎ 02 290351
Netherlands ☎ 02 4855841

HEALTH ADVICE

Sun advice In northern Italy the summers can be hot and visitors should take all the usual precautions against the sun – wearing a hat and suncream, and drinking plenty of water.

Drugs Medicines for personal use only are allowed through customs. Many prescription and non-prescription drugs are available from pharmacies, where you can get excellent advice (often in English). Pharmacies open Monday–Friday 9–12:30, 3:30–7:30, Saturday 9–12:30. If closed, a note displays the location of the nearest pharmacy that is open 24 hours a day.

Safe water Italian water is completely safe, but many visitors prefer the taste of mineral water *(acqua minerale)*, which is readily available.

PERSONAL SAFETY

Italy has two police forces, the Polizia and the Carabinieri. The former is a standard police force, the latter a military-style force that deals with more serious crime. In practice, the visitor will be unable to distinguish between them. Visitors may also see Polizia Stradale, a specific highway force, and Vigili Urbani, which operate within towns.

To help prevent crime:
● Do not carry more cash than you need.
● Do not leave valuables at the poolside.
● Beware of pickpockets in tourist spots or crowded places.
● Avoid walking alone at night in dark alleys in the large cities.
Police assistance:
☎ 113 from any call box

ELECTRICITY

The power supply in Italy is 220 volts. Power sockets are round and two-holed, and take plugs of two round pins. British visitors will need an adaptor and US visitors will need a voltage transformer.

OPENING HOURS

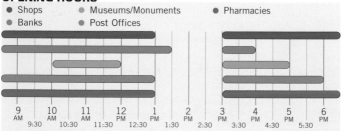

Shops (including pharmacies) sometimes open later in summer. Most shops close Monday morning. Post offices usually open Saturday morning. Museums usually open Sunday morning. Department stores, supermarkets and shops in tourist areas may open outside these times.

Restaurants usually open 12–3, 7–10:30 or 11, but hours can be idiosyncratic and change seasonally. Also, hours are often not as posted.

LANGUAGE

The language you hear on the street will be Italian, even if you are on the Swiss shores of lakes Maggiore and Lugano. There are dialects in the mountains, but even there Italian is the first language. In Italian each syllable is pronounced, so *colazione* would be *col-atz-i-own-ay*. C and g are always 'hard' (as in cat or gate) before *a*, *o* or *u*, and always 'soft' (as in cello or gin) before *e* or *i*. To get a hard c or g before an *e* or *i*, Italians insert an *h*, eg Chianti. *Gn* is pronounced *ny*.

yes	*si*	good afternoon	*buongiorno*
no	*non*	goodnight	*buona sera*
please	*per favore*	how are you ?	*come sta ?*
thank you	*grazie*	do you speak	*parla inglese ?*
welcome	*benvenuto*	English?	
goodbye	*arrivederci*	I don't understand	*non capisco*
good morning	*buongiorno*	how much ?	*quanto costa ?*
bank	*banca*	cheque	*cheque*
exchange office	*cambio*	traveller's	*traveller's*
post office	*ufficio postale*	cheque	*cheque*
coin	*moneta*	credit card	*carta di credito*
banknote	*banconote*	exchange rate	*corse del cambio*
café	*caffè*	beer	*birra*
waiter	*cameriere*	wine	*vino*
waitress	*cameriera*	water	*acqua*
bill	*conto*	coffee	*caffè*
airport	*aeroporto*	boat	*battello*
train	*treno*	ticket	*biglietto*
station	*stazione*	single ticket	*andanta*
bus	*autobus*	return ticket	*andanta e ritorno*
bus stop	*fermata d'autobus*	car	*machina*
hotel	*albergo*	reservation	*prenotazione*
single room	*singola*	room service	*servizio nella stanza*
double room	*matrimoniale*	toilet	*gabinetto*

Best places to see

1 Bellágio

www.bellagiolakecomo.com

The poet Shelley claimed the 'Pearl of the Lake' was the loveliest town not only on Lake Como but in the world, and many since have agreed.

On the narrow road that runs along the eastern shore of the Como arm of Lake Como is a drive that is at best tiring, at worst positively hair-raising. By the time you get to Bellágio you may be too exhausted to notice its beauty. It is also true to say that the approach by road presents the town's poorest aspect. But the approach by water…

Bellágio is at the tip of the Punto Spartivento, the 'point that divides the wind', strung out along a narrow terrace on the western side. As a result, when you arrive by boat, the whole village is laid out for your inspection. The lake front is an array of beautiful buildings, red-roofed and with pastel-shaded walls, above which rises the campanile of the 11th-century church of San Giacomo. At one end of the village is **Villa Melzi,** the finest neo-classical villa on any of the lakes. At the other end, **Villa Serbelloni,** now owned by the Rockefeller Foundation, is equally impressive. Legend has it the villa stands on the site of one of the two residences Pliny the Younger had on the lake.

The villas may be the architectural highlights of the village, but there is much more. Though now possessing a plethora of souvenir shops – many selling locally made silk – and occasionally overcrowded because of its popularity, there is still a real Bellágio beyond the lake-front tourist traps.

Take time to wander through the small maze of steep, sometimes cobbled streets, enjoying both the old-world charm and the occasional stunning views of the lake.

🕀 5B ✉ The point where Lake Como splits into two 🍴 Bilacus (€€), 32 Via Serbelloni; 031 950480 🚌 Buses from Como ⛴ Regular lake boats

Villa Melzi

🕐 Gardens and chapel only, Apr–Oct daily 9:30–6:30 ✋ Moderate

Villa Serbelloni

🕐 Gardens Apr–Oct Tue–Sun. Guided tours only, at 11 and 3:30 ✋ Expensive

2 Duomo, Milan

www.visitamilano.it/turismo_en

Dominating the middle of Milan, and with a forest of statues, the Duomo (Cathedral) is one of the wonders of northern Italy.

On 17 September 1387 a group of Milanese armourers gathered in what is now Piazza Duomo to begin work on the building of a new cathedral for the city. The armourers were followed by the city's

drapers, bootmakers, butchers and others as each craft lent its voluntary efforts to the new building. The Duomo was built of marble from the Candoglia quarry (near Gravellona Toce, close to Lake Maggiore's western shore), the blocks of stone being marked AUF before being shipped by lake, river and canal to the city. The letters stood for *ad usum fabricae* – for building use – as the stone was exempt from local taxes, but so drawn out was the building work that *auf* became a local term for a long wait or for working for nothing. In fact, it was 400 years before the building was completed.

The Duomo Milan is 157m (171 yards) long and 92m (100 yards) wide, the third largest in the world – after St Peter's and Seville Cathedral – and has more than 3,000 statues and spires. At the highest point is the Madonnina, a gilded copper statue of the Madonna. So revered is the statue that by city regulation no building is allowed to rise above it. The Madonnina stands 108m (454ft) above the square and can be viewed at close quarters by those who climb the 919 steps, or alternatively take the lift, to the roof, where the view is superb.

Inside the cathedral, a red light high in the nave marks the position of a True Nail from Christ's cross. It is brought to ground level every year so people can take a closer look. In the crypt lies the body of San Carlo Borromeo, one time archbishop of Milan, whose statue can be seen at Arona (➤ 103).

✚ *Milano 6e* ✉ Piazza Duomo, Milan ☎ 02 86463456
🕐 Mon–Fri 7–7, Sun 1:30–4:30 🖐 Free; Crypt and Treasury moderate 🍴 Al Mercante (€€), Piazza Mercanti 17; 02 8052198 🚇 M1 or M3 Duomo

3 Isola Bella

www.illagomaggiore.com

Some are appalled by the 'wedding cake' of Isola Bella, but many more marvel at the sheer audacity of its creation. Few can stay neutral.

In 1620 the closest to the shore of the three islets off Stresa on Lake Maggiore was rocky and occupied by only a few fishermen and their families. There were two small churches, but it was a hard life for the islanders as there was almost no soil for growing food. At that time, one of the Borromean counts, who owned the islands and much of the nearby mainland, decided to transform the fishing island into a pleasure garden. He died in 1638, but his brother, Count Carlo III, took up his vision.

Carlo had boatloads of soil transported to the island, his architect using it to create a ten-terraced island designed to look, from the shore, like a great ship sailing down the lake. The Count named the island for his wife, Isabella, but the unwieldy Isola Isabella was soon dropped in favour of today's version, which also has the advantage of translating as 'beautiful island'.

On the island the Count and his sons built a vast baroque palazzo, its numerous rooms hung with art

40

treasures. The entire endeavour took decades, and work was not finally completed until 1958. Some of the rooms are exquisite, some exquisitely awful. The Napoleon Room (where he and Josephine slept in August 1797) and the Luca Giordano Room are peaceful and understated; the Great Hall, with its Wedgewood blue walls, is superb; the Tapestry Gallery, with its 16th-century Flemish tapestries, is extraordinary. However, the Music Room is wildly overdone and the grottoes beneath the palace, decorated with shells and curious stucco, are overwhelming, although the collections here are fascinating.

Outside, the gardens are a treasure of overstatement. The statuary of the terraces is appalling, the whole organized in taste so bad it becomes appealing. But the gardens themselves are very good and the views wonderful.

✚ 2C ✉ Offshore from Stresa on Lake Maggiore ☎ 0323 30556 🕐 Apr to mid-Oct daily 9–5 ✋ Expensive (combined ticket with Isola Madre available, €15) 🍴 Elvezia (€€); 0323 30043 ⛴ Regular lake boats from Stresa; boat 'taxis' also available

4 Malcésine

www.visitgarda.com

Viewed from the lake, Malcésine is Garda's most beautiful town, and once you've stepped ashore it only gets better.

Commanding one of the finest views of Lake Garda, Malcésine is a fine prospect itself, rising steeply from its port to a high mass of solid rock topped by a castle. Narrow stone-paved streets wind upwards through archways joining clusters of buildings that date from medieval times, ending at the 14th-century **Castello Scaligero**. This well-reserved pile houses a museum that includes drawings by the German poet Goethe, who was a great admirer of Malcésine. The castle also has medieval frescoes and an open-air theatre in its courtyard that is used for summer performances. Entrance to the castle includes access to its ramparts, and spectacular lake views. A previous castle built on this site by the Longobards was destroyed by the Francs in 590.

At the waterfront, Palazzo dei Capitani is the town's municipal building, formerly the palace of the lake captains. In the lakeside port of Cassone, just to the north, the **Museo del Lago**, opened in 2008, explores the role of the lake in fishing and transport. Outside, two large tanks, fed by the stream dell'Aril (claimed to be the world's shortest river), are filled with eel and fish, revealing the building's original use as a fish hatchery.

Look down on Malcésine and the lake from the Monte Baldo Funivia (➤ 61). In winter skiers ride

it to smaller lifts that extend into the mountain's high snowfields.

✚ 17K ✉ Lake Garda's eastern shore ☎ 045 6570963
🍴 Osteria Alla Rosa (€€), Piazzetta Boccara 5; 045 657
0783 🚢 Regular lake steamers 🚌 Along the eastern lake shore

Castello Scaligero
✉ Via Castello ☎ 045 6570963 🕐 Apr–Nov daily
9:30–6; Dec hours vary; Feb, Mar Sat, Sun 12:30–6
✋ Inexpensive

Museo del Lago
✉ Frazione Cassone 🕐 Apr–Oct Tue–Sun 10–12, 3–6;
Nov–Mar Sun 10–12, 3–6 ✋ Inexpensive

5 Orta San Giúlio

www.orta.net

Set at the bottom of a steep hill and with a marvellous view across Lake Orta, this little village is one of the prettiest on the lakes.

In the fourth century two brothers, Giúlio and Giuliani, arrived at Gozzano, near Lake Orta, to spread the gospel. Giúlio continued to the lake, drawn by the story of evil dragons living on an island at its heart. He amazed the locals by spreading his cloak on the water then stepping onto it, using it as a raft. Giúlio drove the dragons away and stayed on the island, setting up a hermit's cell and preaching to the lake fishermen (▶ 116–117).

The village from which the saint set out is now known as Orta San Giúlio. It is a traffic-free haven with steep streets and picturesque houses, some with external frescoes. One such is the Casa Morgarani, the House of Dwarves, the origin of its name lost in time. The main square, Piazza Motta, is set at the lakeside. It is cool and tree-shaded, and from here you can board boats for the short trip across to the saint's island. There are good restaurants and cafés in the square too.

The village's artistic treasure lies away from the lake, set on the hill above the houses. On the Sacre

Monte a woodland path meanders past 21 chapels that contain almost 400 life-size terracotta statues illustrating scenes in the life of St Francis of Assisi. Work on the chapels and statues began in the 17th century, but the Sacre Monte was not finally completed until early in the 19th century.

✚ 2C ✉ Towards the southern end of Lake Orta's eastern shore 🖐 Free 🍴 San Rocco (€€–€€€), Via Gippini 11; 0322 911977 🚌 Buses along the eastern shore link with southern Lake Maggiore and Gravellona Toce 🛥 Boat from Omegna

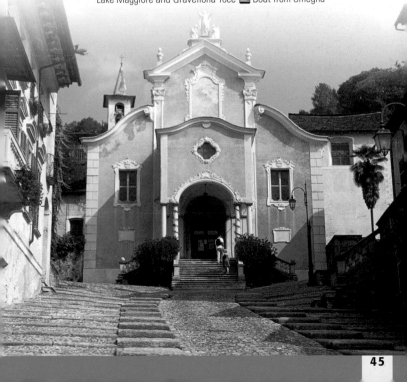

Piazza dei Signori, Verona

www.tourism.verona.it

In the heart of Verona's *centro storico* (historic centre) a perfect Renaissance square reveals the many layers of the city's past.

The entire *centro storico* of Verona has been named a UNESCO World Heritage Site, and it's easy to see why. At the heart of this quarter, and reached through an archway from bustling Piazza della Erbe's daily market, is the serenely elegant Piazza dei Signori.

Two palaces of the medieval Scala family (the Scaligeri), with their characteristic fishtail crenulations, border the square. There is also the 12th-century Palazzo de Ragione (city hall). In

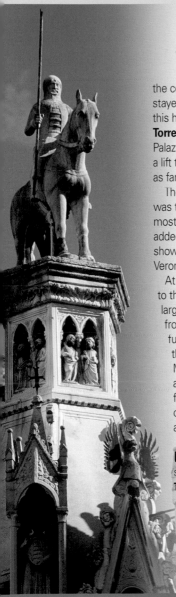

the centre of the piazza is a statue of Dante, who stayed here during his exile from Florence. Above this harmonious ensemble, the slender 83m (275ft) **Torre Lamberti** (Lamberti Tower) rises out of the Palazzo de Ragione. You can climb the tower or ride a lift to the top for bird's-eye views of the city and as far as the Dolomite peaks on a good day.

The frescoed Renaissance Loggia del Consiglia was the last building added to the piazza and is the most ornate. Like the top of the Lamberti Tower, added in the same period, its multi-arched windows show the influence of Venice, which controlled Verona at that time.

At the far end of the piazza, another arch opens to the wildly ornate stone Scaligeri tombs. The largest of the several **Arche Scaligeri**, dating from the 1300s, are topped by stone figures, fully armoured and on horseback. Beside them, the family's church, the 12th-century Santa Marie Antica, seems dwarfed, its interior plain apart from some 13th- and 14th-century frescoes. The tombs are visible through the ornate iron fence, or you can pay admission for a closer look.

✚ 12F ✉ Piazza dei Signori, Verona 🍴 Cafés surround the adjacent Piazza della Erbe

Torre Lamberti

✉ Piazza dei Signori ☎ 045 8032726 🕓 Jun–Sep Tue–Sun 9:30–7:30, Mon 1:30–7:30 ✋ Inexpensive

Arche Scaligeri

✉ Via Arche Scaligeri ☎ 045 595508 🕓 Jun–Sep Tue–Sun 9:30–7:30, Mon 1:30–7:30 ✋ Inexpensive

7 Piazza Vecchia, Bergamo

http://turismo.provincia.bergamo.it

Almost perfectly preserved on its hilltop, Bergamo is one of the finest small medieval cities in Italy.

A *funivia* (a funicular or cable car) connects the modern lower city of Bergamo to the Città Alta, the Upper City, the ancient town set on a hill to the north of the new city. The ride is a short one, no more than a minute or two, but when you step out at the top you have been transported back in time by several hundred years.

Piazza Vecchia – the Old Square – is the heart of the Upper City. The architects Frank Lloyd Wright and Le Corbusier both claimed the square was the finest in Italy dating from the Renaissance. In the middle of the piazza is the Contarini Fountain, given to the city by Alvese Contarini in 1780. Contarini's position as the mayor of Venice explains the

fountain's embellishment with Venetian lions. There is another Venetian lion on the Palazzo della Ragione, the magnificent building at the southern (cathedral) end of the square. The palazzo dates from the last years of the 12th century, making it the oldest municipal hall in Italy (though it needed considerable rebuilding after a fire in the 16th century). Access to the palazzo is by way of the elegant external stairway. The lion on the palazzo is a replica, the original having been torn from the building and smashed in 1796 when the townsfolk were fed up with Venetian rule.

In front of the palazzo is a statue of the poet Torquato Tasso. To the right – as you can see – is the **Torre Civica** (or Torre del Comune), the town's campanile, built in the 12th century, with a 15th-century clock. Climb the tower for a terrific view of the old town. From the Palazzo della Ragione you should cross the length of the square, marvelling at the cunning way brick has been used to create tile-effect paving, to reach the Palazzo Scamozziano, which closes the northern side. This fine building was constructed in the 16th century in Palladian style.

✚ 7D ✉ Bergamo's Upper City 🍴 Colleoni e Dell'Angelo (€€€), Piazza Vecchia 7; 035 232596 🚋 *Funivia* from Viale Vittorio Emanuele II, in the lower city

Torre Civica

☎ 035 247116 🕐 Apr–Oct Tue–Sun 9:30–7 (until 9:30 Sat and hols); Nov–Mar Sat 9:30–4:30 👋 Inexpensive

8 Santa Caterina del Sasso

www.illagomaggiore.com

Apparently clinging to a sheer rock face above the waters of Lake Maggiore, the church of Santa Caterina is one of the most picturesque in Italy.

In the 12th century, the unscrupulous Alberto Besozzi, a local man renowned as a smuggler and money-lender, was crossing Lake Maggiore alone when a vicious storm blew up, capsizing the boat. Besozzi, flung into the water, was in danger of drowning. In terror he promised God that if his life was spared he would repent and live a blameless life of prayer. Miraculously, a wave threw him high onto a ledge on the sheer cliffs near Reno, on the lake's eastern shore. Equally miraculously, he landed uninjured.

Good as his word, Besozzi spent the rest of his life – another 40 years – on the ledge, kept alive by food lowered to him in a basket by people who had heard of the miracle, and water from a spring. When plague threatened the locals, Besozzi prayed for them and they were all spared. In gratitude the locals built a church on the ledge, naming it for Santa Caterina, to whom Besozzi had prayed. When he died, Besozzi was buried in the church.

You can get to the church by boat but if you come by road, you will appreciate the church's unique position as you clamber down the numerous steep steps. (An elevator is currently under construction.) The church at the base was

damaged by a rockfall in the 17th century, but its miraculous nature was further proved when a huge boulder was stopped from demolishing the hermit's tomb by three small bricks that jammed it into a stable position. Built at the very edge of the ledge, the church is a masterpiece of grace and engineering. Inside are beautiful medieval frescoes and the remains of Besozzi – now the Blessed Alberto – curiously preserved from decay.

🚌 2C ✉ Close to the village of Reno on Lake Maggiore's eastern shore ☎ 0332 647172 🕐 Mar–Oct daily 8:30–12, 2:30–6; Nov–Feb Sat, Sun 9–12, 2–5 🍴 Nothing at the site, but on the road to Laveno, a short distance to the north, is Il Porticciolo-Bellevue (€€); 0332 667257 🚢 Regular lake boats

Sirmione

www.visitgarda.com

A finger of land so narrow that it seems an unfeasible site for a town, and a castle from a Hollywood film set combine to create a fairy-tale village.

From Lake Garda's southern shore a finger of land pokes north into the lake waters. The finger is 4km (2.5 miles) long and, at its narrowest, little more than 100m (109 yards) across. At its end is a blob of land – like the dot above an 'i'. On this area of 70ha (173 acres) sits Sirmione. The strategic importance of the isthmus was not lost on those masters of war, the Romans, but the Imperial forces had more than one reason for settling here. Just offshore, from the lake bed about 20m (66ft) below the surface, a thermal spring gushes water at 70°C (158°F). The ruins of the Roman bath house can still be seen. They are called the **Grotte di Catullo,** named for the great lyrical poet Catullus, who had a villa here. The allusion to Catullus may be fanciful but the ruins are worth visiting: A small museum holds local Roman finds. Today the waters of the spring feed a spa that treats muscular ailments and sinus problems.

The isthmus maintained its strategic importance after the Romans departed, and in the 13th century the Scaligeri, lords of Verona, built a castle. Visitors to Sirmione must leave their cars at the apex of the 'i', and walk across a narrow bridge and through a medieval gateway, which gives the impression that

the **castle** itself is being entered. In fact, it stands to the right, complete with a lake-filled moat and an intricate ring of walls that protected supply ships. The walls and towers are topped by the fishtail battlements that were the trademark of the Scaligeri and other medieval families that sided with the Ghibellines against papal power.

➕ 14R ✉ At the southern end of Lake Garda, close to Desenzano 🍴 Trattoria la Fiasca (€€), Via Santa Maria Maggiore 1; 030 9906111 🚌 Buses from Desenzano
🚢 Regular lake boats

Grotte di Catullo
☎ 030 916157 🕐 Apr–Sep Tue–Sun 9–6; Oct–Mar 9–4
✋ Moderate

Scaligeri Castle
☎ 030 916468 🕐 Tue–Sun 8:30–7 ✋ Moderate

10 Villa Carlotta

www.villacarlotta.it

Villa Carlotta is the most famous of the lakes' villas, and with good reason – it's a beautiful villa, elegantly decorated and with superb gardens.

Many visitors arriving here assume the 'C' above the entrance is the 'C' of Carlotta. In fact, it stands for Clerici, the family that built the villa in the 18th century. With its window-pierced façade, symmetry and entrance stairways the villa is a masterpiece. The Clerici sold the villa to the counts Sommariva, and it was during their ownership that most of the art that now graces the villa was collected. Later the villa was sold to a Prussian princess who gave it to her daughter Charlotte (known as Carlotta) as a wedding present. It was Carlotta who laid out the gardens in the 1850s.

Inside the villa the artistic highlight is Antonio Canova's *Cupid and Venus*,

a marvellous portrayal of tenderness. The interior is also notable for its decoration, particularly the ceilings (some based on designs from Pompeii), which are masterpieces of the plasterworkers' art.

For many, though, the gardens are the main attraction. More than 500 species of trees and shrubs grow here, as well as ferns and flower beds. There are about 150 varieties of rhododendron and azalea, many of them in Azalea Avenue or trimmed to create hedges. There are also large collections of camellias and wisterias. In summer, the flowers and shrubs make Carlotta the most vivid place on the lakes, while the citrus trees add a sharp tang to the air.

➕ 5B ✉ Tremezzo, on the western shore of Lake Como ☎ 0344 40405 🕐 Apr–Sep daily 9–6; Oct 9–5; last two weeks in Mar, first two weeks in Nov 9–12, 2–4:30 ✋ Expensive 🍴 Alberghetto della Marianna (€€), Via Regina 57, Cadenabbia di Griante; 0344 43095 🚌 Buses along the shore road from Como 🚢 Regular boat service

Best things to do

Great places to have lunch

Al Mercante (€€)

In an amazingly quiet and picturesque square just a short distance from the Duomo. Eating outside on a sunny day captures the flavour of medieval Milan.

✉ Piazza Mercanti 17, Milan ☎ 02 8052198

Bilacus (€€)

Reserve your table in advance as this is the most popular place in town – and rightly so. Dining on the terrace, with the lake beyond and the hustle of the street below, is excellent, as is the food.

✉ Via Serbelloni 32, Bellágio ☎ 031 950480

Colleoni e Dell'Angelo (€€€)

Outstanding. The restaurant is on an old and exquisite palazzo. The service and cooking are equally good.

✉ Piazza Vecchia 7, Bergamo (Upper City) ☎ 035 232596

Da Candida (€€)

Very atmospheric, with traditional furnishings that match the traditional dishes on the menu.

✉ Via Marco 4, Campione d'Italia ☎ 091 6497541

Fioroni (€€)

Dine on the terrace overlooking Lake Como's narrow southern arm and enjoy lake fish, lamb chops or a bountiful mixed grill.

✉ Strada a Lago, Carate Urio ☎ 031 400149

La Laconda dell'Isola (€€)

An extraordinary place with a set menu that has not varied for years. A little awkward to reach, but well worth the effort.

✉ Isola Comacina, Lake Como ☎ 0344 56755/55083

La Peschiera (€€)

Fresh lake fish served in sight of the lake. Excellent value for the food, the price, the view…

✉ Via Lungo Lago, Isola dei Pescatori ☎ 0323 933808

Il Porticciolo-Bellevue (€€€)

One of the best restaurants on the lake, tucked away on the eastern shore of Lake Maggiore, close to the church of Santa Caterina del Sasso. The terrace has magnificent views. Specializes in lake fish, but has a good selection of alternative dishes.

✉ On the lakeside road 2km (1.25 miles) south of Laveno ☎ 0332 667257

Sacro Monte (€€)

One of the best restaurants on Lake Orta, in a traditionally furnished and beautifully set building, which adds to the ambience. Excellent menu and cooking.

✉ Via Sacro Monte 5, Lake Orta ☎ 0322 90220

Trattoria Al Porto (€€)

It's not just the charming surroundings of the historic restaurant that makes it so popular. It's the traditional – but very unusual – way of preparing lake fish; order *tinca al forno con polenta* and prepare for a real treat.

✉ Porto del Pescatori 12, Clusane, Lake Iseo ☎ 030 989014

Places to take the children

LAKE MAGGIORE AND LAKE LUGANO
Funivia to the Mottarone

The cable car offers a great ride, and a great view, though unfortunately there is limited potential for walking at the top.

✉ Piazza Stazione 1, Stresa ☎ 0323 30399; www.stresa-mottarone.it ⏱ Daily 9–5:30 ✋ Moderate

Museo del Cioccolato (Chocolate Museum)

Watch chocolate being made and taste the end product.

✉ Caslano ☎ 091 6118856; www.alprose.ch ⏱ Mon–Fri 9–5:30, Sat, Sun 9–4:30 ✋ Inexpensive

Villa Pallavicino

The park has a zoo with 40 animal species, most of which are free to roam. Children can get close to the more docile animals.

✉ Via Sempione 61, Stresa ☎ 0323 32407/31533; www.parcozoopallavicino.it ⏱ Daily 9–6 ✋ Expensive

Zoo Safari del Lago Maggiore

A safari park with lions, tigers, giraffes, white rhinos, camels and more. There is also an aquarium with fish from Lake Maggiore and, in case it all seems a bit tame, piranhas.

✉ Just off SS (Stradale Statale) 32 (Arona-Novara) at Pombia, about 15 minutes drive from Arona ☎ 0321 956431 ⏱ Daily 10–7 (11–4 winter) ✋ Expensive

LAKE COMO
Castello Vezio

A real medieval castle for kids to explore while parents enjoy the ceramics workshop and woodcarvings in the artisans' shops.

✉ Perledo (near Varenna) ☎ 348 8242504; www.castelldivezio.it

🕓 Mar–Oct daily 10–6 ✋ Moderate

LAKE GARDA
Acquapark Altomincio

Superb park with an array of water slides, some awesomely long and breathtakingly fast. Good facilities for younger children.

✉ Valeggio Sul Minicio ☎ 045 7945131 🕓 Late May–early Sep daily 10–7 ✋ Expensive

Caneva World

Two sites: Aqua Paradise, which is largely water-based with slides, pools and rides, and Movie Studios with sets from films.

✉ Via Fassalta 1, Lasize (very close to Gardaland) ☎ 045 6969700; www.canevaworld.it 🕓 May–Sep daily 10–7 ✋ Expensive

Gardaland

Gardaland has everything, with gigantic roller coasters and numerous water rides topping the bill.

✉ Castelnuovo del Garda, near Peschiera del Garda ☎ 045 6449777; www.gardaland.com 🕓 Apr to mid-Jun daily 10–6; mid-Jun to mid-Sep 10am–11pm; mid-Sep to Oct Sat, Sun 10–6 ✋ Expensive

Monte Baldo Funivia

Kids should love the revolving cable car up Monte Baldo. At the top, easy trails follow the mountain ridge, known for its wild flowers.

✉ Via Gardesana ☎ 045 7400206 🕓 Apr to mid-Sep daily 8–7; mid-Sep to mid-Oct 8–6; mid- to late Oct 8–5; Nov–Mar hours variable ✋ Moderate

Parco Natura Viva

A safari park that also has full-size models of dinosaurs.

✉ Loc. Figaro 40, Bussolengo, near Pastrengo, to the east of Lazise ☎ 045 7170052 ✋ Expensive

a drive around the Intelvi Valley

In Como, follow the road with the lake to your right, past traffic lights, then turn right onto the road to Switzerland. At the top of the hill turn right, back towards the lake, then take the road that bypasses the lakeside villages. Near Argegno, turn left for Schignano/Erbonne/Cerano.

Schignano is not a single village but a collection of scattered hamlets. Erbonne lies at the end of a long road and is just a short distance below the Swiss border. In the middle of the village is the old communal wash house.

Wind uphill for lovely views of the lake. Go through Santa Anna and follow the signs for Casasco, through Schignano, to the boundary sign for Cerano d'Intelvi. Pass the church, then turn left for Casasco/San Fedele/Veglio. Follow this road to a junction (intersection) and turn right. At the next T-junction, in San Fedele d'Intelvi, turn left along a road signed for Lanzo, Porlezza and Switzerland. The road passes through the twin villages of Pello d'Intelvi (Inferiore and Superiore). Go through Scaria to reach Lanzo, then bear right at the Hotel Milano for the funivia down to Santa Margherita, an Italian village on Lake Lugano's southern shore. Return to Hotel Milano and bear right for Sighignola. Past Lanzo d'Intelvi, drive along Via Sighignola, climbing through pretty woods to reach Sighignola itself.

At Sighignola, there is a fabulous viewpoint and an uncompleted *funivia* to Campione d'Italia. Enjoy the magnificent view of Lake Lugano, Monte Rosa and the Alps before reversing the drive to Lanzo.

In the square, bear right – with the Cristal Bar to your left – to reach a junction (intersection). Turn left, then right shortly after, for Como, going through Castiglione d'Intelvi and descending to the lake at Argegno. Turn right to return to Como.

Distance 105km (65 miles)
Time 4–5 hours
Start/End point The lake front, Como ✚ 4C
Lunch La Tenda Rosa ✉ Via Laino 2b, San Fedele d'Intelvi
☎ 031 831225 ⏰ Tue–Sun

Top activities

Windsurfing
The winds that blow across the lakes are highly dependable, particularly at the northern ends. Add the sun and warmth and the area is ideal for water sports. Windsurfing is the most popular of these. Torbole, on Lake Garda, is one of Europe's leading centres.
Conca Windsurf ✉ Lungolago Verona, Torbole ☎ 0464 548192; www.windsurfconca.com
Vasco Renna Professional Surf Center ✉ Parco Pavese 1, Torbole ☎ 0464 505993; www.vascorenna.com

Sailing
Sailing is almost as popular as windsurfing, and clubs at smaller towns and villages offer classes on a variety of boat types.
L'Associazione Nautica Sebina ✉ Via Industriale 5, Località Ambrosa, Sulzano, Lake Iseo ☎ 030 985732, 030 985196
Surfsegnana Porfina Beach ✉ Viale Rovereto 100, Riva del Garda ☎ 0464 505963; www.surfsegnana.it

Diving
The lake waters are not exceptionally clear, but the lack of tides is a bonus for those learning to dive.
Aquatica Equipment hire, PADI courses, guided dives ✉ Via Foro Boario 21, Arco (northern Lake Garda) ☎ 0464 510366; www.ambienteacqua.com

Swimming
Swimmers should take care as they are not highly visible from a windboard or boat.

Skiing
There are numerous possibilities in winter – the Alps to the west of Lake Maggiore, the pre-Alps closer to the lake; the Grigna and Resegone peaks above Lake Como and the Alps north of the lake; the high peaks that form the back walls of the Bergamo valleys; and the ridges of Lake Garda, especially Monte Baldo (➤ 42).

Climbing and canyoning

The Grigna peaks and the mountains north of Riva del Garda, around Arco, are famous for their rock-climbing. Deep canyons have been carved in fantastic shapes by rivers filled with melting mountain snow.

Cavalcalario Outdoor Club ✉ Bellágio, Lake Como ☎ 339 5308138; www.bellagio-mountains.it

Guide Alpine SEB1 ✉ Via del Cantiere 15a, Lóvere, Lake Iseo ☎ 035 983733; www.seb1.it

Canyon Adventures ✉ Via Matteotti 5, Torbole, Lake Garda ☎ 334 869 8666; www.canyonadv.com

Golf

With the climate and the magnificent views from some of the local courses, the visitor with an enthusiasm for golf is well catered for. Tourist information offices have a list of clubs.

Mountain biking

Piedmont, Lombardy and Trentino have all produced booklets of suggested itineraries for mountain bikers, and bicycles and guides can be easily hired. The northern end of Lake Garda is a popular destination for adventure enthusiasts.

Iseo Bike ✉ Campeggio del Sole, Iseo ☎ 340 3962095; www.iseobike.com

GardaOnBike ✉ Via Matteotti, Torbole ☎ 0464 550880; www.gardaonbike.com

Walking and trekking

The ridges that define the lake valleys are excellent for walking, with several long-distance trails and day walks. The harshest terrain is in the Val Grande near Lake Maggiore, on the Grigna peaks above Lake Como and on Monte Baldo, on Lake Garda's eastern shore. Easier walking is on the lower ridges.

Stunning views

TOP VIEWS FROM THE LAKES

- The town of Bellágio (➤ 36–37)

- The church of Santa Caterina del Sasso (➤ 50–51)

- The town and castle of Malcésine (➤ 42–43)

- The town of Sirmione (➤ 52–53)

- Isola San Giúlio (➤ 116–117)

GREAT VIEWS FROM ABOVE THE LAKES

Scenic routes

LAKE MAGGIORE
Centovalli by train
One of Europe's most scenic train rides leaves the lake shore in Locarno by vintage rail cars to explore the Centovalli (100 valleys), riding high above the Melezza River and its tributaries, each of which has carved a valley of its own.

✉ Leaves from Locarno's rail station ☎ 091 756 0400; www.centovalli.ch

Mottarone Funivia
From the minute the cable car leaves the lakeside, a wonderfully changing series of views begins, first over the Borromean Islands

and finally, at the top, a 360-degree panorama that includes Lake Orta.
✉ Piazza Statione, Stresa ☎ 0323 30399
🕐 Daily 9–5:30 ✋ Moderate

Shore drive from Palanza to Locarno
As Lake Maggiore blends from Italy into Switzerland, it becomes more closed in by mountains that frame pretty waterside villages.

LAKE LUGANO
Lugano to Porlezza by boat
The narrow arm of Lake Lugano that stretches eastwards into Italy is the lake's most scenic part. The changing views of the lake and the villages that cling to its wooded shore, backed by mountains, are best seen from the water.
Boat trips ✉ Società Navigazione Lago di Lugano ☎ 091 971 52 23; www.lakelugano.ch

Sentiero dell'Olivo path
Stroll through olive groves along the sloping shore of Lake Lugano from Lugano's flower-filled Parco degli Olivi to Gandria, the most picturesque of the little villages that cling to the steep shore.

LAKE COMO
Como to Bellágio by boat (► 130)
Drive through the Intelvi Valley (► 62–63)
The Lake Como Greenway (► 132–133)

LAKE GARDA
Drive through the Tremósine (► 171)
Malcésine to Riva del Garda by boat (► 162)

Exploring

With the Alps to the west and north, the Dolomites to the east, and the plain of the River Po to the south, the Italian Lakes occupy an enviable position. Abundant water from the mountains, and equally abundant sunshine have created ideal growing conditions, allowing the establishment of world-famous gardens. The equable winter climate brought the rich and famous, whose villas added to the architectural and artistic richness of an area already wealthy because it lay on the trade route from Venice to northern Europe. With fine cities and towns, an array of delightful villages, fine Italian cooking, and endless opportunities for water and other sports, the Italian Lakes are among the most interesting and exciting destinations in Europe. And to cap it all, just a short distance south is Milan, economic powerhouse of Italy and fashion capital of the world.

Milan

Milano

Milan, Italy's second city but its unquestioned economic hub, deserves a book of its own. There is a Roman city, *Mediolanum*, named after its position at the heart of the Lombardy Plain. Then there is the city whose early Christian monuments rival those of any other town. There is the Milan of the Viscontis and Sforzas, that of the Spanish domination and another from the Austrian era. There are marvellous palazzos from the 18th and 19th centuries and the modern commercial city. There is even the Milan whose soccer teams are the equal of any in Europe and whose stadium at San Siro is worth visiting just to be amazed at its size and elegance.

Which of these cities should be explored by the visitor on a time budget? Perhaps a little of each, the 'must-see' sights, which are covered here. As with all large, commercially active cities, Milan can be all pace and movement. But at its heart, in Piazza Duomo and the nearby squares, the Italians find, as always, time for a coffee and a moment's relaxation away from the hustle.

 5E

BASILICA DI SANT'AMBROGIO

Legend has it that Ambrogio (St Ambrose) arrived in Milan soon after the city's bishop had died. The contest for a successor was causing feuding and uproar. Ambrogio calmed the crowd, and they were so impressed with his bearing they decided he should be the new bishop. Ambrogio was not even a Christian at the time, but was hastily baptized and installed as bishop. Soon after, he began work on the church that now bears his name. The present church, a lovely building in Romanesque style, dates from the 11th century although there are sections of much earlier work. Inside, the gold altar by Volvinio, with its relief panels depicting scenes in the life of the saint, is a masterpiece of ninth-century goldsmithing.

✚ *Milano 2e* ✉ Piazza Sant'Ambrogio ☎ 02 86450895 ⏰ Tue–Sun 9:30–12, 2:30–6 ✋ Free 🚇 M2 S Ambrogio

BIBLIOTECA (PINACOTECA) AMBROSIANA

The vast Palazzo dell'Ambrosiana was begun in the early 17th century to house the library of Cardinal Federico Borromeo, a member of the family that owned, among other things, the islands in Lake Maggiore. The building is a little severe, but inside is an excellent collection of art, and the library. The collection has works by Brueghel, Caravaggio and Luini, but is most notable for the portrait of the musician Gaffurio by Leonardo da Vinci.
www.ambrosiana.it

✚ *Milano 5e* ✉ Piazza Pio XI. Near to Piazza Duomo ☎ 02 806921 ⏰ Tue–Sun 10–5:30 ✋ Expensive 🚇 M1 or M3 Duomo

CASTELLO SFORZESCO

The first castle on this site was built by the Viscontis from the mid-14th century. This building was partially destroyed by the townsfolk on the downfall of the family, but their joy must have been short-lived as the Sforzas soon rose to power and created an even more domineering structure. The Sforza fortress fell into disrepair but was saved from demolition by enlightened citizens and now

houses superb collections of art, weapons and armour, and much more. Of the art, pride of place must go to the awesome *Rondanini Pietà* by Michelangelo, while the collection of weapons is one of the finest in Europe. The castle is also worth visiting just for the building itself. Look up as you enter the Torre dell'Orologio, the Clock Tower. This superb 70m (230ft) tower is an exact replica of the 15th-century original destroyed when the gunpowder stored within exploded.

www.milanocastello.it

✚ *Milano 3c* ✉ Piazza Castello ☎ 02 88463700 ⏱ Summer daily 7–7; winter 7–6 🚇 M1 Cairoli ✋ Free

DUOMO
Best places to see, ➤ 38–39.

MUSEO NAZIONALE DELLA SCIENZA E DELLA TECNOLOGIA LEONARDO DA VINCI

The museum named after Leonardo houses not only an excellent collection exploring science and engineering but a gallery dealing with his work in aeronautics, engineering and anatomy. The 'conventional' section of the museum includes full-size ships, planes and trains, and exhibits such as the equipment used by Umberto Nobile on his balloon-borne expedition to the North Pole.

www.museoscienza.org

✚ *Milano 1e* ✉ Via San Vittore 21 ☎ 02 485551 ⏰ Tue–Fri 9:30–7, Sat, Sun 9:30–6:30 👛 Expensive Ⓜ M2 S Ambrogio

PINACOTECA DI BRERA

Palazzo di Brera was begun in the early 16th century and is in fine baroque style with a unity that belies the fact that it took more than 100 years to complete. In the courtyard is a bronze statue of Napoleon by the artist Canova. This fine work is a prelude to the collection inside, which many consider one of the best in Italy. Everyone will have a favourite, but by common consent the finest works are the heartbreaking *Dead Christ* by Andreas Mantegna; and the *Madonna with Saints*, which includes the famous portrait of Federico di Montelfeltro (and his equally famous nose) by Piero della Francesca.

www.brera.beniculturali.it

✚ *Milano 5b* ✉ 28 Via Brera ☎ 02 722631

🕐 Tue–Sun 8:30–7

♨ Expensive 🚇 M2 Lanza

SANTA MARIA DELLE GRAZIE

In 1463 the Dominican Order of friars was given land on which to
build a church and monastery. The church, dedicated to St Mary of
the Favours, is built in dramatic style with a marvellous façade and
apse. It has two surviving cloisters, the Cloister of the Dead and
the smaller Cloister of the Frogs. The church is well worth visiting,
but its famed treasure, Leonardo da Vinci's *Last Supper*, is within

the nondescript building beside it, once the refectory. The artist began work on the painting in 1495. Always the innovator, he chose to paint onto dry plaster rather than using the more common technique of painting quickly onto wet plaster. This allowed him more time – it took two years to complete the work – but meant that moisture between the plaster and the paint lifted flakes of paint off the wall. Within 20 years the painting had begun to deteriorate. There have been several attempts at restoration, the most recent, lasting 21 years, ending in 1998. It is hoped that this one has permanently stabilized the masterpiece. Da Vinci's composition places the apostles in groups of three, often considered to be a symbolic reference to the Holy Trinity. Unlike most late 15th-century depictions of the scene, he includes Judas on the same side of the table as the other eleven apostles.

www.grazieop.it

✚ *Milano 1d* ✉ Cenacolo Vinciano (Da Vinci's *Last Supper*), Piazza Santa Maria delle Grazie 2 (Corso Magenta 1) ☎ 02 92800360 🕐 Tue–Sun 8–7.30 ✋ Church free. *Last Supper* expensive 🚇 M1 Conciliazione ❓ Booking a time to see the fresco is obligatory (by phone or online)

VILLA REALE (VILLA BELGIOJOSO BONAPARTE)

Built in neoclassical style and once owned by Napoleon, the Villa Reale, at the edge of Milan's Public Gardens, is now the city's museum of modern art. The rooms are a marvel of 18th-century elegance, with chandeliers, parquet floors and sumptuous plasterwork, to such an extent that the works, from the late 19th and early 20th centuries, can seem a little out of place. Many are by north Italian artists, but there are also paintings by Cézanne, Renoir, Gauguin, Picasso and Matisse. After exploring the museum, go to the back of the villa. The rear façade is by far the best and can be viewed across a delightful lake.

www.gam-milano.com

✚ *Milano 8b* ✉ Via Palestro 16 ☎ 02 76340809 🕐 Daily 9–5.30 ✋ Free 🚇 M1 Palestro

a walk around Milan's highlights

Start in front of the Duomo (➤ 38–39) in Piazza Duomo.

Facing the Duomo, bear right to walk along the side of the building. This is Via Arcivescovado, though you will not see this displayed. To the right is Palazzo Reale.

Palazzo Reale must not be confused with Villa Reale (➤ 79). It was once the Ducal Palace of the Viscontis and was partially destroyed by fire but renovated and added to over the years. Mozart's first opera was performed here when he was 14 years old. The *palazzo* houses the Museo del Duomo, a collection of religious objects.

Continue along the road, on the right is San Gottardo with its beautiful campanile. Turn left behind the cathedral. To the right is the Palazzo Arcivescovile, built in 1170, while ahead is Piazza Fontana. At the end of the cathedral, turn left to return to the main square. Turn right through the Galleria Vittorio Emanuele.

The Milanese refer to the Galleria as *Il salotto di Milano*, the drawing room of Milan, because its cafés and restaurants are traditional meeting places. The exclusive Savini's is where crowds assemble after the first night at La Scala.

Exit the Galleria into Piazza della Scala. The opera house is to the left. Ahead is a statue of Leonardo da Vinci.

Walk on, with Palazzo Marino to the right, then turn right to reach one side of the church of San Fedele. Step right into Piazza San Fedele.

San Fedele is the most complete of Milan's 16th-century churches. It was built by San Carlo Borromeo (➤ 103) and outside is a monument to Alessandro Manzoni (➤ 141).

Go back to the side of the church and bear left across the road to reach the Casa degli Omenoni.

Casa degli Omenoni is the House of Giants, named after the eight caryatids sculpted on the outside by Leone Leoni, for whom the house was built in 1565.

Continue past the House of Giants (along Via degli Omenoni), to Piazza Belgioioso, turning left along it.

Palazzo Belgioioso was built for a family whose name is carved in the piazza outside. Farther on, to the left, is a museum in Manzoni's home from 1814 until his death.

Continue along Via Gerollamo Morone from the end of the square to reach Via Alessandro Manzoni. Turn right towards the Poldi-Pezzoli Museum.

In a fine 17th-century palazzo, this is one of Italy's foremost museums. Art includes *Profile of a Young Woman* by Pollaiolo and works by Luini, Mantegna and Botticelli.

Turn left along Via Alessandro Manzoni, soon reaching Piazza della Scala again.

La Scala opera house was built in 1778, taking its name from the Scaligeri family. In its early days the theatre was mostly used as a gaming house but its reputation was transformed with the rise of Verdi. Today La Scala is one of the world's great opera houses. There is a **museum** about the theatre.

Pass the theatre, crossing Via Santa Margherita, Via San Protaso and the tram lines of Via Tommaso Grossi. Go under the arch and across the pedestrianized road to Piazza dei Mercanti.

On the street side is the Palazzo della Ragione, its arcaded lower floor once a market, its upper storeys the town hall and law courts. Opposite is the Palazzo delle Scuole Palatine, a 17th century school of mathematics, rhetoric and law, beside the 14th-century marble Loggia degli Osii.

Now take the few steps back to Piazza Duomo.

Distance 2km (1.25 miles)
Time 1–3 hours, depending on museums visited
Start/End Point In front of the Duomo, in Piazza Duomo
✚ *Milano 6e*
Lunch Al Mercante (€–€€) ✉ Piazza Mercanti 17 ☎ 02 8052198; www.ristorantealmercante.it 🕐 Mon–Sat lunch and dinner
Museo del Duomo ✉ Piazzo Duomo ☎ 02 860358; www.duomomilano.it 🕐 Daily 9:30–12:30, 3–6 💷 Inexpensive
Casa del Manzoni ✉ Via Morone 1 ☎ 02 86460403; www.casadelmanzoni.mi.it 🕐 Tue–Fri, Sun 9–12, 2–4 💷 Free
Museo Poldi-Pezzoli ✉ Via Manzoni 12 ☎ 02 794889; www.museopoldipezzoli.it 🕐 Tue–Sun 10–6. Early closing Sun afternoons (summer) 💷 Expensive
Museo Teatrale alla Scala ✉ Piazza della Scala ☎ 02 88797473; www.teatroallascala.org 🕐 Daily 9–12:30, 1:30–5 💷 Moderate

HOTELS

Albergo Giulio Cesare (€€)
A small and recently renovated hotel, close to the Duomo and central sights. Rooms are plain, but well equipped, with telephones, air conditioning and private bathrooms.
✉ Via Rovello 10, 20121 Milano ☎ 02 72003915; www.giuliocesarehotel.it

Cavour (€€)
Situated in a fashionable part of town, and only a short distance from the heart of Milan. Some of the rooms have balconies with city views.
✉ Via Fatebenefratelli 21, 20121 Milano ☎ 02 620001; www.hotelcavourmilan.com

Grand Hotel et de Milan (€€€)
Almost off the price scale, with all possible facilities. Situated next to La Scala, within a short walk of the Duomo. Two excellent restaurants. Opera lovers should request the suite where composer Giuseppe Verde lived for several years and composed some of his operas.
✉ Via Manzoni 29, 20121 Milano ☎ 02 723141; www.grandhoteletdemilan.it

Hotel Sanpi Milano (€€€)
This small boutique hotel is within walking distance of the Centrale train station in the Corso Buenos-Aires/Porta Venezia shopping area. The exceptionally accommodating staff and the hotel's striking architecture make it a stand-out.
✉ Via Lazzaro Palazzi 18, 20124 Milano ☎ 02 29513341; www.hotelsanpimilano.it

Manzoni (€€)
This hotel is just off Via Montenapoleone, so you won't have too far to carry the shopping bags. There are good facilities, but no restaurant.
✉ Via Santo Spirito 20, 20121 Milano ☎ 02 76005700; www.hotelmanzoni.com

RESTAURANTS

NB: Be aware that many restaurants in Milan close during August.

4 Mori (€€)
Just across from the entrance to the castle. In summer you can dine in the garden, but the restaurant is often crowded.
✉ Largo Marie Callas 1 ☎ 02 878483 🕔 Mon–Fri lunch and dinner, Sun lunch 🚇 M1 Cairoli

Alfredo-Gran San Bernardo (€€€)
Probably the best place for true Milanese cooking. Try the risottos and the *cotoletta Milanese*. Worth the journey and the bill.
✉ Via Borgese 14 (near the Fiera – the international fair area) ☎ 02 3319000; www.alfredogransanbernardo.it 🕔 Lunch and dinner

Al Girarrosto (€€)
Traditional Tuscan cooking in elegant surroundings close to the Duomo.
✉ Corso Venezia 31 ☎ 02 76000481 🕔 Mon–Fri lunch and dinner, Sat, Sun dinner 🚇 M1 San Babila or Palestro

Al Mercante (€–€€)
Beautifully sited just a step away from the Duomo. Excellent menu and alfresco eating in a Renaissance market square. One of the most romantic restaurants in the city.
✉ Piazza Mercanti 17 ☎ 02 8052198; www.ristorantealmercante.it 🕔 Mon–Sat lunch and dinner 🚇 M1 or M3 Duomo

Antico Ristorante Boeucc (€€€)
Dine in elegant surroundings at one of the oldest restaurants in the city. The emphasis is on traditional northern-Italian dishes.
✉ Piazza Belgioioso 2 ☎ 02 76020224; www.boeucc.com 🕔 Mon–Fri lunch and dinner, Sat, Sun dinner 🚇 M1 or M3 Duomo

Bagutta (€)
Lovely little restaurant a bit off the beaten track, to the north of San Babila. Eat on the terrace and enjoy a place of great character as

well as good food. The restaurant specializes in Tuscan dishes.
✉ Via Bagutta 14 ☎ 02 7600092; www.bagutta.it 🕐 Lunch and dinner
Ⓜ M1 San Babila

Biffi Scala (€€€)

Gualtieri Marchesi, the first chef in Italy to get three Michelin stars,
has taken over this classic Milan restaurant near La Scala.
✉ Piazza della Scala 8 ☎ 02 866651 🕐 Mon–Fri lunch and dinner, Sun
dinner. Closed early Jul Ⓜ M1 or M3 Duomo

Da Ilia (€€)

For more than half a century this family has been serving comfort
foods to appreciative locals; near the Public Gardens.
✉ Via Lecco 1 ☎ 02 29521895; www.ristorante-ilia.it 🕐 Mon–Fri lunch,
dinner, Sat, Sun dinner Ⓜ M1 Porta Venezia

Don Lisander (€€–€€€)

A great place to eat in summer, when you can dine in the beautiful
garden. Good international menu, which changes regularly.
✉ Via Manzoni 12 ☎ 02 76020130 🕐 Mon–Sat lunch and dinner Ⓜ M1 or
M3 Duomo

Frijenno Magnanno (€–€€)

Calzone and pizza are the specialities here, and they do them well.
Handy for Stazione Centrale, where good food is hard to find.
✉ Via Benedetto Marcello 93 ☎ 02 29403654 🕐 Tue–Sun 11–11 Ⓜ Caiazzo

Giannino (€€€)

Typical Milanese cooking in a lovely setting. Delightful rooms and
an exquisite garden for alfresco eating in summer.
✉ Via Sciesa 8 ☎ 02 55195582 🕐 Mon–Sat lunch and dinner

Il Giardino di Giada (€€)

This is one of the best Chinese restaurants in the city. The quality
menu always includes one 'budget' meal.
✉ Via Palazzo Reale 5 ☎ 02 8053891; www.giardinodigiada.it 🕐 Tue–Sun
lunch and dinner Ⓜ M1 or M3 Duomo

Gocce di Mare (€€)

Very elegant restaurant. Ideal for continuing the fish experience of the lakes as it has one of Milan's best fish menus.

✉ Via Petrarca ☎ 02 4692487 ⏰ Mon–Fri lunch and dinner, Sat, Sun dinner Ⓜ M1 Conciliazione

Joia (€€€)

There's a bit of meat and fish on the menu, but mostly this restaurant caters creatively to vegans and vegetarians, with beautiful presentations that tempt carnivores, as well.

✉ Via Castaldi 18 ☎ 02 29522124; www.joia.it ⏰ Mon–Fri lunch and dinner, Sat dinner Ⓜ M3 Republica, M1 Porta Venezia

La Nôs (€€)

This is a delightful place, elegant and often with a piano player. It's one of the few Milanese restaurants with parking, and there'a an excellent Lombard menu.

✉ Via Bramante 35 ☎ 02 3315363 ⏰ Wed–Sun lunch and dinner, Tue dinner Ⓜ M2 Moscova

Savini (€€)

Savini may have the priciest café seats in town, but it's definitely the place to be seen. Don't bother looking for a table here after the curtain falls at La Scala opera house, when Milan society moves in en masse.

✉ Galleria Vittorio Emanuele ☎ 02 72003433; www.savinimilano.it ⏰ Mon–Fri lunch and dinner, Sat dinner Ⓜ M1 or M3 Doumo

La Tavernetta-da-Elio (€)

Known for its meat dishes, this Tuscan restaurant is a bit out of the way, but is a favourite with locals. The most popular dish is the *Bistecca alla Fiorentina* – young beef grilled Florentine style.

✉ Via Fatebenefratelli 30 ☎ 02 653441; www.tavernetta.it ⏰ May–Oct Mon–Fri lunch, dinner, Sat dinner Ⓜ M3 Turati

Trattoria all'Antica (€)

In the Naviglia district of the city, but well known for serving

excellent food at reasonable prices and so justifiably popular.
✉ Via Montevideo 4 ☎ 02 8372849 🕓 Apr–Oct Mon–Sat lunch, dinner
Ⓜ M2 San Agustino

L'Ulmet (€€€)

A great, if expensive, place in winter, when a welcoming fire burns
away in the hearth. Superb menu and very pleasant surroundings.
✉ Via Disciplini, corner of Via Olmetto ☎ 02 86452718; www.lulmet.it
🕓 Tue–Sat lunch and dinner, Mon dinner Ⓜ M3 Missori

SHOPPING

Milan's Fashion Quarter, the Quadrilatero della Moda, is for
browsing only, unless your annual income runs to more figures
than you have fingers. But window-shopping is irresistible. Within
this district, bordered by Via Montenapoleone (Montenapo to
locals), La Spiga, San Andrea and Manzoni, you'll find every name
in high fashion, from Armani and Chanel to Valentino and Versace.
The district is said to have the world's highest concentration of
designer shops.

The Quadrilatero is, of course, not the only shopping area, nor is
alta moda the city's only claim to retail fame. Corso Buenos-Aires
is one of Europe's largest shopping streets, with that edgy Milano
look at more realistic prices. Covered galleries of boutiques branch
off Corso Vittorio Emanuele between Piazza San Babila and Piazza
del Duomo, where you can enter Galleria Vittorio Emanuele II, its
shops still as elegant and rarefied as they were when it opened
nearly 150 years ago.

Head to Via Torino for shoes and for clothes with a younger look.
At its end, the Ticinese district is the place to find small speciality
shops and craftsmen's studios. So is Navigli, farther on, where a
street market along the canal sells antiques and collectibles on the
last Sunday of each month. More antiques mix with clothing and
accessory shops in the streets around Pinotaca Brera. For leather
shops, go to Via Canonica, in the Paolo Sarpi area.

Look for off-price designer fashions in outlets at 50–70 per cent
off; secondhand *haute-mode* occasionally turns up at street
markets such as the Saturday morning market at Viale Papiniano.

Designer shops aside, we've listed below a selection of Milan's best stores.

FASHION
10 Corso Como
Off-price outlet with out-of-season *alta moda* for men and women.
✉ Via Tazzoli 3 ☎ 02 29015130; www.10corsocomo.com
🚇 M2 Garibaldi FS

Outlet 2000
High-quality women's knitwear outlet.
✉ Via Marghera 24 ☎ 02 4815768 🚇 M1 Fiera Milano

La Rinascente
A department store that is more like a collection of classy speciality shops.
✉ Piazza Duomo ☎ 02 8852275 🚇 M1 or M3 Duomo

Il Salvagente
Top-name designer labels at deep discounts.
✉ Via Bronzetti 16 ☎ 02 76110328; www.salvagentemilano.it

I Santi
Leather factory outlet that sells off-price handbags and accessories.
✉ Via B Corio 2 ☎ 02 5416 981 🚇 M3 Porta Romana

FOOD
Peck
One-stop shop for Italian food specialities to bring home, from dried porcini and Parma ham to jars of chestnut cream.
✉ Via Spadari 9 ☎ 02 8023161; www.peck.it 🚇 M1 or M3 Duomo

GIFTS
La Piccola Legatoria
Choose from a range of notebooks, paper-covered boxes and nicely designed paper.
✉ Via Palermo 11 ☎ 02 861113; www.lapiccolalegatoria.it 🚇 M2 Lanza

ENTERTAINMENT

CLUBS
Check the websites to find out which night to go to which club, as the whole scene changes nightly – and dress stylishly.

Alcatraz
In an old industrial building and serving up a mix of industrial-strength live music and alcohol.

✉ Via Valtellina 21 ☎ 02 69016352; www.alcatrazmilano.com 🚇 Maciachini

Blue Note
Intimate live-jazz club with big-name artists.

✉ Via Borsieri 37 (Piazza Segrino) ☎ 02 69016888; www.bluenotemilano.com
🚇 M2 Garibaldi FS

Club Hollywood
Everyone who is anyone comes here at some time, eagerly watched by the paparazzi.

✉ Corso Como 15 ☎ 02 6598996; www.discotecahollywood.it 🚇 Garibaldi FS

Divina
House music from popular local DJs attracts the crowds.

✉ Via Molino delle Armi at Via della Chiusa ☎ 02 58431823 🚇 M3 Missori

Magazzini Generali
Dance club and 900-seat venue for roadshows.

✉ Via Pietrasanta 14 (Ripamonti) ☎ 02 55211313

CONCERT/OPERA VENUES
FilaForum
Big-name international shows play here.

✉ Via G di Vittorio ☎ 02 53006501 ❓ Get tickets from Ticket One (www.ticketone.it) or Easy Tickets (www.easytickets.it)

Teatro alla Scala
Perhaps the world's greatest opera house (➤ 82).

✉ Piazza La Scala ☎ 02 861827; www.teatroallascala.org 🚇 Duomo

Western Lakes

Close to Mont Blanc there is a mountain peak (Mont Dolent) where France, Switzerland and Italy touch. From it, the high ridge of the Alps heads northwestwards and eastwards and the country borders follow it. The Matterhorn lies on the border between Switzerland and Italy, as does Monte Rosa. From Monte Rosa the high ridge and the border turn northeast towards the Simplon Pass. On the Italian side of the ridge the land falls away swiftly – it is barely 60km (37 miles) from the second-highest summit in the Alps to the edge of the Lombardy Plain.

Lago Maggiore

Lago di Lugano

Varese

This is the Italian region of Piemonte (Piedmont), a name that translates, accurately, as the foot of the mountains. The whole of Lake Orta and the western shore of Lake Maggiore lie within the region, the eastern shore lying in Lombardy. Border crossings are usually very relaxed, but it is always wise to carry your passport with you. Also, be sure to carry insurance documents for your car as occasionally the border police will ask for them and they have been known to refuse entry to drivers who don't have them.

Lake Lugano

Lugano is a strangely shaped lake, more like a series of lakes joined together as it winds its way back and forth between Italian and Swiss shores. The city of Lugano and the northern shore of the lake were once part of the city state of Milan, but the Swiss took the city and adjacent land in 1512 and, despite the common language and the oddity of Campione, no serious attempt has ever been made to regain the northern shore. As a result, Italian Lake Lugano is fragmented: There is a small section of the southwestern shore, the enclave of Campione and a larger section of the eastern lake. The best way to see the more scenic eastern part of the lake is on one of the frequent lake steamers.

 4B

CAMPIONE D'ITALIA

In the eighth century the local lord of this part of Lake Lugano gave in perpetuity the land which is now Campione to the church of Sant'Ambrogio in Milan. Remarkably, when the Swiss annexed Milanese holdings on the northern shores of the lake they respected the original covenant and made no attempt to take the village that had grown up on the church's holding. During the struggles of Austrian rule over parts of north Italy and the wars of the Risorgimento, Switzerland made no attempt to absorb the village. And so, despite the fact that the village – which has now grown into a town – is entirely surrounded by Switzerland, it remains resolutely Italian. Of necessity, Campione uses the Swiss postal system and all the shops and restaurants accept Swiss money, but this is very much an Italian town. A plan to link the town with Italy by building a cable car from it to Sighignola, a small village near Lanzo d'Intelvi (➤ 63), failed so Campione's unique position, reachable only from Switzerland, will continue for many years. The town now makes the most of its position by having a **casino.**

Visitors to Campione are left in little doubt about the unusual nature of the town when they are greeted by a huge arch and elaborate fountain. In medieval times the town was famous for the Maestri Campionesi, a group of architects, builders and sculptors who were renowned for the quality of their work. The group built Sant'Ambrogio in Milan, Modena Cathedral and the more modest, but no less beautiful, church here. Most visitors reach Campione by one of the frequent boats from Lugano, although it is possible to drive there.

✚ 4B ✉ An Italian enclave on Lake Lugano's eastern shore 🚌 Infrequent buses from Switzerland 🚢 Regular lake steamers 🍴 Da Candida (€€), Via Marco 4; 091 6497541

Casino

✉ Campione d'Italia ☎ 091 6401111; www.casinocampione.it 🕓 Daily, restaurant open at 12, gaming tables at 3pm

PONTE TRESA

Unsurprisingly, Ponte Tresa is the bridge that crosses the Tresa river, the outflow of Lake Lugano flowing west to Lake Maggiore. The bridge, a five-arched, red granite structure, is also the border between Italy and Switzerland, and so there are actually two towns, both called Ponte Tresa. Italian Ponte Tresa is usually a traffic bottleneck – ignore the traffic chaos and park early to enjoy the lake front on the eastern side of the village, a delightful area. Take a stroll around the rest of the village and peruse its shops.

✚ 4B ✉ At the western end of Lake Lugano's southern shore

PORTO CERESIO

Following two sides of a square-cut bay of Lake Lugano, Porto Ceresio is a lovely place. The village is renowned for the views along the two arms of Lugano and across the lake to Morcote, but

don't ignore Porto Ceresio itself. There is nothing of great note here, just a huddle of pretty houses and the little harbour of the same name, but it encapsulates the quiet elegance of the less 'touristy' lakes. From the village a road heads south towards Varese, soon reaching Besano, a village famous for the local rocks, which are one of Italy's most important sources of Triassic fossils – there is a small **fossil museum.** Farther along, the same road leads to Bisuchio, where the 16th-century Villa Cicogna Mozzoni is a national monument. The villa has an arcaded ground floor and important frescoes, and stands in Italian-style gardens.

🞧 4C 🖂 Close to the Swiss border on the southern shore of Lake Lugano

Museo Paleontologico

🖂 Via Prestini 5, Besano 🖂 0332 919200 🕓 Apr–Sep Tue–Fri 10–12:30, Sat, Sun 11–12:30, 2:30–6:30; Oct–Mar Tue–Thu 9:30–12:30, Sun 2:30–6:30 ✋ Inexpensive 🚍 Buses from Varese

Swiss Lake Lugano

A large portion of Lake Lugano lies in the Italian-speaking Swiss
canton of Ticino. The elegant, modern city of Lugano makes a good
base for exploring the lovely scenery and towns nearby.

LUGANO

Most of Lugano's highlights lie close to the lake. At the southern
end of the city is Paradiso, a suburb of new hotels, good

restaurants, nightclubs and shops. A funicular climbs from a station here, offering panoramic views from Monte Salvatore. Heading north, you are soon in the old quarter of the city. Here, the church of Santa Maria Degli Angioli has some of the best frescoes by Bernardino Luini, pupil of Leonardo and, some maintain, the equal of his master. From the church, follow Via Nassa north. The surrealist sculpture in Piazzetta San Carlo is *The Dignity of Time* by Salvador Dalí. Via Nassa leads to Piazza della

Riforma, with its cafés and the impressive town hall. The square is one of the main venues for Lugano's famous Jazz Festival each June. Cross to the lakeside and continue towards Parco Civico. Inland from it is Quartière Maghetti, a modern district of shops and restaurants. On the edge of the Quartière, the **Museo Cantonale d'Arte** displays contemporary art and the work of all Swiss, but chiefly Ticino, artists.

Another funicular climbs Monte Bré, a good starting point for walks. A walking path, the Sentiero dell'Olivo (➤ 68), leads to Gandria, with its delightful **Smuggling Museum**.
➕ 4B

Museo Cantonale d'Arte
✉ Via Canova 10 ☎ 091 9104780; www.museo-cantonale-arte.ch
🕐 Wed–Sun 10–5, Tue 2–5 💷 Expensive

Smuggling Museum (Museo Doganale Svizzero)
✉ Gandria ☎ 091 9104811 🕐 Apr–Oct daily 1:30–5 💷 Moderate

MELIDE AND SOUTH OF LUGANO

Heading south from Lugano there are several interesting places on the lake's northern shores. At Melide, the **Swissminiatur** is a replica of the main sights in Switzerland set out on an area of 1ha (2.5 acres). From Melide a *funivia* (cable car) takes you to Carona, where there is a fine park and a church with 16th-century frescoes. Farther on, Morcote is often called the 'Pearl of the Lake'. With its narrow streets of arcaded houses and the beautiful setting of the church of Santa Maria del Sasso among tall cypresses, it is easy to see why. Elsewhere on the peninsula of land that ends at Morcote, admirers of the writing of Herman Hesse can make a pilgrimage to Gentilino, where he is buried. Farther from Lugano, across the lake at Capolago, a **rack-and-pinion railway** takes you to the top of Monte Generoso, a much higher peak. From the top, walkers can explore an alpine landscape rich in wild flowers.

✚ 4C

Swissminiatur

✉ Melide ☎ 091 6401060 🕓 Daily mid-Mar to late Oct 9–5:30 (Fri–Sun sometimes until 10) ✋ Expensive 🍴 There is a café at the site

Rack-and-Pinion Railway to Monte Generoso

✉ Capolago ☎ 091 6305111 🕓 May–Oct daily 9:15–7:15 ✋ Expensive 🍴 Café at the top (€)

VALLE DI MUGGIO

The mountains between lakes Lugano and Como form a land apart, one foot in Switzerland, one in Italy, part 21st-century, part caught in ways of a century ago. The innovative **Museo Etnografico della Valle di Muggio** captures this ambiguity, with sites scattered throughout the valley. Begin at the information centre in Cabbio for an overview, then visit the chestnut-drying shed and public laundry fountain up the street before taking the 30-minute walk to the Mulino di Bruzella. This stone mill has ground local red corn into polenta for the past 300 years. The miller demonstrates the process and you can buy this rare polenta.

✚ 4C

Museo Etnografico della Valle di Muggio

✉ Casa Cantoni, Cabbio ☎ 091 6902038 ⏰ Apr–Oct Tue–Sun 2–5. Mulino di Bruzella Thu, 1st and 3rd Sun 2–4

Lake Maggiore

As with Lake Lugano, you will find that to do a full circuit of the lake you will need to take your passport with you, as such a trip will cross into and out of Switzerland. At a distance of 170km (105 miles), a full circuit is rather too far to travel in a single day if justice is to be done to the places along the way.

✚ 3B

ANGERA

This small town tucked into a cove of Lake Maggiore's southeastern shore has a lovely lake-front walk shaded by chestnut trees. The **Museo Civico Archeologico** explores the town's interesting history, noting that Pietro Martire, the chronicler of Columbus's journey to the New World, was a local man. Though

the town is pleasant, most visitors come to see the forbidding *rocca* (castle) that looms above it – visit the town by boat for a real appreciation of just how impressive and well situated this formidable fortress really is. It was built by the Borromean family in the 15th century and was cleverly designed to ensure that attacks invariably turned the attackers' unprotected right side towards the defenders. Inside it is unfurnished, its gaunt appearance adding to its sinister qualities, though some rooms have surprisingly subtle frescoes. The castle is now the home of an excellent **doll museum**, which concentrates on European dolls from the 19th century to the present day.

✚ 2C

✉ At the southern end of Lake Maggiore's eastern shore 🍴 Bacco (€€), Via Mazzini 71; 0331 930232

Museo Civico Archeologico

✚ Palazzo Pretorio, Via Marconi 2 ☎ 0331 931133
🕐 Mon, Thu, Sat 3–7 🎟 Free 🚌 Regular buses along the eastern shore ⛴ Regular lake boats

Castle and Doll Museum

✉ Rocca Borromea ☎ 0331 931300;
www.borromeoturismo.it 🕐 Apr to mid-Oct daily 9–5:30 🎟 Expensive 🍴 None on site, but lots of choice in the town

ARONA

Across the lake from Angera, Arona owes its prosperity to the age of railways, as it stands at the point where the line from Switzerland through the Simplon Tunnel meets the line linking Milan to Turin. This economically strategic position is reflected in the array of fine 19th-century houses. One older building, the Palazzo de Filippi, houses a **museum** that explores the town's history. Arona's castle, **La Rocca**, faced Angera's across the lake, and its ruins still provide a good vantage point. Several churches reflect the town's importance: Collegiata di Santa Maria, Santa Maria di Loreto and Santi Martiri, reached by a long staircase.

Just outside Arona stands the colossal **statue of San Carlo Borromeo.** The saint was born in Arona Castle in 1538, was appointed Cardinal at 22 and was Archbishop of Milan by the time he was 26. Though the fact that his uncle was Pope Pius IV may have helped his promotion, he was undoubtedly a devout and hard-working man. The statue is 23.5m (77ft) tall, stands on a plinth 12m (40ft) high, and is apparently a good likeness of the man, right down to his huge nose. Visitors can climb up within for a precarious view from inside the head, but since the statue is made of bronze it can be very hot in summer.

✚ 2C ✉ At the southern end of Lake Maggiore's western shore

Museo Archeologico

✉ Piazza San Graziano ☎ 0322 48294; www.archeomuseo.it 🕐 By request only 🖐 Free 🍴 Pescatori (€€), Via Marconi 27; 032 248312 🚍 Infrequent buses along the western shore 🚤 Regular lake boats

La Rocca (castle remains)

✉ Above the town to the west ☎ 0322 243601 🕐 Apr, May daily 2–5; Jun–Oct daily 10–7:30 🖐 Free 🚍 No buses, so a car or taxi is required to reach La Rocca

Statue of San Carlo Borromeo

✉ North of Arona ☎ 0322 249669 🕐 Mar–Sep daily 9–12:30, 2–6:30; Oct, Nov daily 9:30–5 🖐 Inexpensive 🚍 Regular buses along the western shore 🚤 Regular lake boats

BORROMEAN ISLANDS

Offshore from Stresa on Lake Maggiore's western shore lie three small islands. The most famous of these is Isola Bella (➤ 40–41), but the other two are also worth visiting.

Isola Bella

Best places to see, ➤ 40–41.

Isola Madre

The largest island, and the one furthest from Stresa, is Isola Madre, the Mother Island. Here the Borromeo family built a single villa, landscaping the parkland around it. The villa is decorated in a much more subdued and relaxed style than its neighbour on Isola Bella. The chapel beside it houses the tombs of many members of the Borromeo family, reflecting the fact that Madre was a place where the family lived rather than where they impressed their rivals. The island's parkland is a treasure house of rare species, including a Kashmir cypress, said to be the finest specimen in Europe. There are also rows of citrus plants scenting the air, and a tropical greenhouse.

🕂 2C ✉ Offshore from Stresa and Pallanza ☎ 0323 31261 🕓 Easter–Oct
daily 9–12, 1:30–5:30 💰 Expensive 🍽 La Piratera (€€), Isola Madre; 032
331171 🚢 Regular lake boats from both Stresa and Pallanza ❓ Visitors
cannot land on the island unless they purchase an entry ticket

Isola dei Pescatori

This, as the name implies, is the fisherman's island, the only one
of the Borromean trio that reflects the original occupation of the
islands. While the Borromeo family was transforming Isola Bella
and laying claim to Isola Madre for their private villa, Pescatori was
owned by the Archbishop of Novara, who refused to give it up. It is
a marvellous place with fishing boats – the traditional *lucia* with
which all visitors to the lakes soon become familiar – at the
harbour edge and nets hung over the walls to dry in the sun.
The island is entirely occupied by a village that is achingly
picturesque and, apart from the area where boats drop visitors,
free of souvenir shops. At the heart of the village is the
11th-century church, with its neat conical spire.

🕂 2C ✉ Offshore from Stresa 🍽 Ristorante Belvedere (€€), Via di Mezzo;
0323 32292 🚢 Regular boats from Stresa

CÁNNERO RIVIERA

Cánnero was once described as the 'Genoese Riviera in miniature', a fact that prompted the town fathers to add Riviera to the name and to style it as the 'Nice of Maggiore' because of the mildness of its winter climate. It was also described as 'a pearl in a bracket of villas and vineyards', a description that is much less appropriate today as the vineyards have all but gone. The villas remain, though: In one, Villa Sabbioncella, Garibaldi stayed after the battle of Luino during his Risorgimento campaign. Neither that villa nor any other is open to visitors, who must content themselves with an exploration of the huddle of narrow streets, each lined with fine houses. All explorations are likely to end at the little harbour, from which there is a view of the two small Cánnero or Malpaga islands, each of which is topped by the ruins of a castle. The

castles date from the 12th century and were once occupied by a band of five brothers who terrorized the local villages and pirated any ship unfortunate enough to come too close. Eventually the Viscontis became fed up with this blatant display of lawlessness, though it took them six months to force the brothers out of their strongholds before destroying the castles.

🚌 3B ✉ On the western shore of Lake Maggiore to the north of Verbania 🍴 Il Cartile (€€), Via Massimo d'Azeglio 73; 0323 787213 🚌 Regular bus service along the western shore 🚢 Regular lake steamers

CANNÓBIO

Though sadly split in two by the main road up Maggiore's western shore, Cannóbio is still worth a visit. On the lakeside, narrow, picturesque streets lead to the Santuario della Pietà, which houses a painting that allegedly started bleeding in 1522. The chapel is the work of Pellegrini, a famous 16th-century architect who was commissioned by San Carlo Borromeo himself, the two men's involvement an

indication of the effect the miracle had on the area. On the mountain side of the main road, a minor road reaches the *orrido* of Sant'Anna. An *orrido* is a tight gorge through which a noisy stream rushes, in this case the Torrente Cannóbio, which reaches the lake at the town. Close to the gorge is the neat church after which it is named.

🚌 3B ✉ The first town in Italy if travelling south from Switzerland along Lake Maggiore's western shore 🍴 Sant'Anna (€€), at the *orrido;* 0323 70682 🚌 Infrequent bus service along the western shore 🚢 Regular lake steamers

LAVENO

Visitors who use the car ferry to cross Lake Maggiore
from Verbania are treated to a magnificent view of
Laveno, which is dominated by the church of Santi
Giacomo e Felipe, built only in the 1930s and on a
very grand scale. Those arriving by boat will also note
the curious yellow buckets that travel slowly up the
hillside behind the town. They are the transporters of
one of the lakes area's most exciting *funivias* (a type
of cable car). Each car carries two people (standing).
The gate is securely fixed but there is no other
protection in most cars, although covers have
recently been added to a few. Although you may
need nerves of steel to take this ride, it does allow a
good view of the brightly hued butterflies that
congregate along the swathe of scrub cut through the
forest below the *funivia*. The view from Sasso del
Ferro at the top is magnificent.

✚ 3C ✉ On Lake Maggiore's eastern shore 🚌 Infrequent
buses along the eastern shore 🚢 Regular lake steamers.
Car ferry (which takes foot passengers) from Verbania

Funivia

☎ 0332 668012; www.funiviedellagomaggiore.it 🕐 Apr–Sep daily 9:30–6
(Sat, Sun and holidays until 7); Oct–Mar Sat, Sun and holidays 9:30–5
✋ Moderate 🍴 Ristorante a Monte (€–€€), at the cable-car summit;
0332 610303

LUINO

This delightful small town has two claims to fame. It was the first
place in Italy to raise a statue in honour of Giuseppe Garibaldi, the
hero of the Risorgimento. Garibaldi came to the town to raise
another army after he had been defeated by the Austrians at the
battle of Custozza. This event, and other aspects of the town's
history, are explored in a **museum** in Palazzo Verbania. The statue

stands in Piazza Garibaldi (of course) where, on Wednesdays, a market is held. The second claim is that the great artist Bernardino Luini was born here. A painting of the *Adoration of the Magi* in the church of San Pietro – at the eastern, uphill section of the town – is attributed by some experts to the artist. In the church of Madonna del Carmine beside the main lakeside road are frescoes that are the work of pupils of Luini.

🕂 3B ✉ On Lake Maggiore's eastern shore 🚌 Infrequent buses along the eastern shore 🚢 Regular lake steamers 🍴 Trattoria Tre Re (€€), Via Manzoni 29; 0332 531147

Museo Civico di Luino

✉ Palazzo Verbania ☎ 0332 532057 🕓 Wed 8–12, 2:30–6:30 🖐 Free

PALLANZA

Pallanza is just one of three villages – the others are Intra and Verbania – which make up the community shown on maps as Verbania. The other two villages form a commercial town and ferry port (Lake Maggiore's only car ferry links Verbania to Laveno), but Pallanza is sufficiently removed to maintain a degree of individuality.

The old village has the usual maze of narrow streets lined with fine houses. It has a long-standing reputation as an autumn and winter resort, and as a place where the flowers and shrubs seem to bloom even more vividly than elsewhere. The latter led to the village being referred to as the 'cradle of flowers' in old guides to the lake. Pallanza as a resort is mentioned in the classic Hemingway book *A Farewell to Arms*, where the characters planned 'to go to Pallanza. It is beautiful there when, in autumn, the leaves change their colour…There is a nice village at Pallanza and you can row out to the islands where the fishermen live…'

Palazzo Dugnani, a fine 18th-century building in the old quarter, is now the **Museo del Paesaggio,** with a collection of landscape paintings and frescoes. Just outside the village is **Villa Taranto,** a garden of 16ha (40 acres) beside the road that links Pallanza with Verbania. One of the world's great gardens, the villa's grounds are

criss-crossed by 8km (5 miles) of paths and shelter more than 20,000 varieties of trees and shrubs from all over the world. Some of these specimens are the only examples in Europe. There are also ponds and a greenhouse with rainforest plants. In spring the garden's

Tulip Week, when over 80,000 tulips are in bloom, gathers crowds from all over the world. A little later in the season, the blooming of the azaleas and rhododendrons is another highlight.

➕ 2B ✉ Part of the Verbania complex of towns/villages on Lake Maggiore's western shore 🍴 Il Torchio (€€), Via Manzoni 20; 0323 503352 🚌 Infrequent buses along the lake's western shore 🚢 Regular lake steamers

Museo del Paesaggio

✉ Via Ruga 44 ☎ 0323 556621; www.museodelpaesaggio.it 🕐 Apr–Oct Tue–Sun 10–12, 3.30–6:30 🖐 Incxpensive

Villa Taranto

☎ 0323 404555 🕐 Gardens only Mar–Oct daily 8:30–6:30 or sunset 🖐 Moderate

SANTA CATERINA DEL SASSO

Best places to see, ➤ 50–51.

STRESA

Stresa is the most elegant of all Lake Maggiore's towns, its lakeside gardens are evidence of a prosperity mirrored in the array of substantial hotels. Of these hotels, the finest is the very grandly (if curiously) named Grand Hotel et des Iles Borromées, one of just two on the lakes that lie outside the Italian hotel classification system because they are too luxurious merely to be five-star (the other is the Villa d'Este at Cernobbio on Lake Como). It was in this hotel that Hemingway had Frederick Henry stay to escape the war in *A Farewell to Arms*. It is interesting that for being so elegant and

famous a town – Stresa has a renowned annual music festival and is frequently home to conferences – it is such a tiny place and has so few attractions within its boundaries. There are some good shops and the usual souvenir outlets; and Piazza Cadorna, the central square, with its outdoor cafés, is excellent, but that is all. The town is a fine base for local excursions, though.

To the north is the lower station of the *funivia* to the Mottarone, from which there is a view of Monte Rosa. On clear days Milan's Duomo and the Matterhorn are visible. The *funivia* makes a stop at the **alpine garden** near Gignese, where thousands of species of alpine flowers have been planted since 1934. From the garden there is a splendid view of the lake. Beyond the *funivia,* Baveno is a very pleasant village with a 12th-century Romanesque façade and campanile. Beside the church is a baptistery with 15th-century frescoes. Baveno became a socialite resort after Queen Victoria stayed for a week in 1879. South of Stresa is **Villa Pallavicino.** The 19th-century villa is not open to the public, but its 12ha (30 acres) of parkland is. Here, there are formal gardens, but the most entertaining feature is the safari-style zoo, with the animals in minimal caging and good access for children to the docile species.

🚩 2C ✉ On Lake Maggiore's western shore 🍴 Piemontese (€€), Via Mazzini 25; 0323 30235 🚌 Frequent tourist 'trains' from Stresa to Villa Pallavicino 🚢 Regular lake steamers

Giardino Alpino

✉ Gignese ☎ 0323 31308; www.giardinoalpino.it 🕐 Apr–Oct Tue–Sun 9:30–6 ✋ Inexpensive

Villa Pallavicino

☎ 0323 31533; www.parcozoopallavicino.it 🕐 Mar–Oct daily 9–6 ✋ Expensive

Swiss Lake Maggiore

The northern end of Lake Maggiore lies in Switzerland. Visitors who head north along the western shore will cross the border soon after leaving Cannóbio.

ASCONA

Isadora Duncan, Herman Hesse and Paul Klee all spent time here, as did Lenin and Jung. The town's lake front is traffic-free, allowing visitors to savour it in peace. Ascona is separated from the larger, better-known town of Locarno by the wide Maggia river. Those with time to spare can follow the Valle Maggia to reach Ponte Brolla – the starting point of the enchantingly named Val Centovalli or the Valley of a Hundred Valleys, which is fine walking country.

⊞ 3A ✉ Close to Locarno 🚌 Regular buses from Locarno
🚢 Regular lake steamers

LOCARNO

Locarno wraps itself around a sheltered inlet of the lake which, because it faces southwest and faces the lower hills, gets many hours of sunlight. The lake front and nearby squares are alive with bright flowers and pleasant outdoor cafés. Inland from the lake, past the Kursaal Casino, the **Castello Visconti** is now a museum of local archaeology. At the heart of the old town is Piazza Grande, with its shops and restaurants. If you head north from it, along Via della Stazione, you will come across the lower station of a *funivia* (cable car). This leads to the 15th-century church of Madonna del Sasso, with superb views of the lake and the cable car, then a chairlift that rises to 1,672m (5,485ft). Elsewhere in the town, the Casa Rusca in Piazza Sant'Antonio, a fine 17th-century house, has a tradition of being occupied by artists, and holds regular exhibitions of work by contemporary painters and sculptors.

⊞ 3A

Castello Visconti

✉ Via Castello 2 ☎ 091 7910091 🕐 Apr–Oct Tue–Sun 10–12, 2–5
✋ Moderate 🍴 Villa Pauliska (€€), Via Orselina 6; 091 7430541

Lake Orta

By comparison to the lakes to the east, Orta is just a splash of water, yet at 14km (9 miles) long, 3km (2 miles) wide and 143m (470ft) deep it would be a large lake in other locations.

✚ 1C

ISOLA SAN GIÚLIO

Visitors staying in Orta San Giúlio (➤ 44–45) who rise with the sun and look out across the lake are sometimes treated to a rare sight. A thin, dense layer of mist lies on the water, waiting for just a little more sunlight before it rises and disperses, and above it, seemingly floating on a cloud, is Isola San Giúlio. A similar, more easily observed but less striking view can be seen each night

when buildings on the island are floodlit and seem disembodied against the dark waters of the lake and the mountains beyond.

On the island, the church dedicated to the founding saint is the finest Romanesque building in the area. Built in the ninth century on the site of San Giúlio's hermit cell, it has many treasures. The black marble pulpit is 11th century, the carved lecterns and walnut choir stalls are masterpieces and a silver urn holds the remains of Giúlio himself. A section of bone from one of the dragons the saint displaced (➤ 44) is probably a whale bone. Beside the church the 14th-century Palazzo dei Viscovi is now a monastery.

✚ 1C ✉ Island off Orta San Giúlio at the southern end of Lake Orta

🍴 Limited on the island, but lots of choice in Orta San Giúlio (€–€€€)

🚢 Regular lake steamers or water 'taxis' from Orta San Giúlio

MADONNA DEL SASSO AND LAKE ORTA'S WESTERN SHORE

Lake Orta's western shore is steep, the road which links the hillside villages narrow and twisting. But there are worthwhile places to visit. The highlight is the church of Madonna del Sasso, perched on a granite outcrop close to the village of Boleto. The church has some interesting artwork, including fine 18th-century frescoes and a 17th-century crucifix, but is most notable for the view from it, which takes in virtually the entire lake.

Closer to Omegna are the upper and lower Quarna villages (Quarna Sopra and Quarno Sotto). They have a history of producing fine work in wood and brass and are also famous for making musical instruments. There is a small **museum of instruments** and their manufacture in Quarna Sotto, which is open during the summer.

✚ 1C

Museum of Musical Instruments

✉ Quarna Sotto ☎ 0323 89622; www.museoquarna.it 🕐 Jul–Sep daily 10–12, 3–7 💰 Inexpensive 🍴 Little locally, but good choices in Omegna

🚌 Infrequent buses from Omegna

OMEGNA

With a population of about 16,000, Omegna is Lake Orta's largest town. It is a pleasant place, still retaining part of its 13th-century wall, though it is more industrialized than most of the other places on the lake. The ruins of an ancient bridge across the river still provoke debate between those experts who date its origins to the time when the town was Roman Vomenia, and those who detect more recent (but still medieval) work. Close to the lake front is the town's old quarter, with some beautiful old houses, many still with

their outside stairways and wrought ironwork, with balconies and shutters. Be sure to find time to visit the church of Sant'Ambrogio, which has an excellent 16th-century polyptych.

✚ 2C ✉ At the northern end of Lake Orta, straddling the lake's outflowing river 🍴 La Conchiglia (€€), Via IV Novembre 187; 032 362317 🚌 Buses from Gozzano and Gravellona Toce 🚢 Regular lake steamers

ORTA SAN GIÚLIO
Best places to see, ➤ 44–45.

VARESE AND SURROUNDINGS

The large, modern city of Varese is built on flat land below Monte Campo dei Fiori. It is a prosperous place, famous for its shoe making, but with other light industries and a reputation as a 'garden city' because of its parks and the lushness of the local valleys.

Within the city, which is worth visiting for its wealth of modern shops, be sure to see Del Bernascove, the campanile, 72m (236ft) high, that stands at the heart of the old town and is a symbol of Varese. There is an interesting complex of religious buildings beside the campanile. One, the 12th-century baptistery of San Giovanni, is a national monument. Nearby, the baroque Palazzo Estense is another national monument. It was built in the mid-18th century by Francesco II Este, Duke of Modena, and is situated in an extensive natural park, fronted by formal gardens.

From Varese, you can visit Monte Campo dei Fiori for a view of the picturesque village of Santa Maria del Monte, or explore the local lakes and valleys. Lake Varese is the largest of the three lakes between the city and Lake Maggiore. On the lake's island, Isolina Virginia, excavations have revealed prehistoric remains of enormous importance. Of the valleys, the Valganna, which takes the main road to Ponte Tresa, is the most scenic, with small lakes and fine woodland, but the

Valcuvia – between Varese and Lake Maggiore – is the most interesting. From the Valcuvia a side road climbs steeply to **Arcumeggia,** where, from the 1950s, contemporary artists have frescoed the outside walls of the houses to create an open-air art gallery. The works are not of the highest quality, perhaps, but the idea is great fun.

South of Varese, Castiglione Olona should be visited to see one of Lombardy's most important **complexes of medieval buildings.** In the early 15th century Cardinal Branda Castiglioni, a local man, built a palazzo for himself, a house for his parents, a domed church, a baptistery and a collegiate church. He commissioned the master artist Masoline de Panicale to paint frescoes on the churches and baptistery. There is a small museum devoted to the history of the site.

✚ 3C

Arcumeggia

✉ At the top of a steep road from the Valcuvia; car or taxi essential, but parking can be difficult ☎ 0332 283604

Church Complex/ Museum

✉ Castiglione Olona. On the N233 (Milano) road south of Varese ☎ 0331 858301
🕐 Tue–Sun 9–12, 3–6 💰 Moderate
🍴 Colombo Rosella (€€), Via Cesare Battisti 112, Castiglione Olona; 0331 859275
🚌 Infrequent buses

HOTELS

LAKE ORTA

L'Approdo (€€)
The hotel makes the most of its small-town setting with a fine garden giving lake and mountain views and an excellent restaurant.
✉ Corso Roma 80, 28028 Pettenasco ☎ 0323 89345 ⏰ Jun to mid-Feb

San Rocco (€€–€€€)
Beautifully converted from a 17th-century convent, with elegant rooms overlooking the lake and island (which guests can visit by private launch); outstanding dining room and personal service.
✉ Via Gippini 11, 28016 Orta San Giúlio ☎ 0322 911977;
www.hotelsanrocco.it

Santa Caterina (€)
About 2km (3 miles) to the east of the town, with surprisingly stylish rooms for its price point. No restaurant.
✉ Via Marconi 10, 28016 Orta San Giúlio ☎ 0322 915865;
www.orta.net/s.caterina ⏰ Mid-Mar to Oct

LAKE MAGGIORE

Beau Rivage (€–€€)
Well-situated in one of the best villages for a base on the western shore, the hotel has excellent facilities and a good restaurant.
✉ Viale della Vittoria 16, 28831 Baveno ☎ 0323 924534

Camin Hotel Luino (€€)
A bit pricey for Luino, but a beautifully restored Libery-style (art nouveau) villa with a good restaurant. Very comfortable and has an excellent restaurant with a lake terrace.
✉ Viale Dante 35, 21016 Luino ☎ 0332 530118; www.caminhotelluino.com

Conca Azzurra (€€)
In a village just north of Angera. Tidy little hotel with a pool, sports facilities and a restaurant.
✉ Via Alberto 53, 21020 Ranco ☎ 0331 976526; www.concazzurra.it
⏰ Mid-Feb to mid-Dec

La Fontana (€€)

A little north of Stresa, set back from the lakeside road in pretty grounds, well shaded by trees. No restaurant but a pleasant walk to Stresa's many options.

✉ Via Sempione Nord 1, 28838 Stresa ☎ 0323 32707; www.lafontanahotel.com 🕒 Jan to mid-Nov

Giardino (€)

Very pleasant and well located, with excellent facilities and a good restaurant.

✉ Corso della Repubblica 1, 28041 Arona ☎ 0322 45994; www.giardinoarona.com

Grand Hotel et des Iles Borromées (€€€)

One of the great hotels of the lakes area, offering gardens, views of the Borromean Islands and an excellent restaurant

✉ Corso Umberto I 67, 28838 Stresa ☎ 0323 938938

Grand Hotel Majestic (€€€)

In a stunning location on a promontory, surrounded by water and gardens, this four-star hotel deserves both the 'grand' and 'majestic' in its name.

✉ Via Veneto 32, 28922 Pallanza ☎ 0323 509711; www.grandhotelmajestic.it

Serenella (€€)

Small hotel with friendly hosts and a good dining room, in a lakeside village north of Baveno, perfectly located for exploring Maggiore and Orta.

✉ Via Quarantadue Martiri 5, Feriolo, north of Baveno ☎ 0323 28112; www.hotelserenella.net

Verbano (€€)

A romantic hotel on Pescatori island. Guests have the island to themselves when the crowds go home. Facilities include a restaurant.

✉ Via Ugo Ara 2, 28838 Isola Pescatori ☎ 0323 30408; www.hotelverbano.it

LAKE LUGANO
Albergo L'Ancora (€)
Lovely little hotel in a beautiful village beside Lake Lugano. Very good restaurant.
✉ Via Mazzini 3, 21050 Porto Ceresio ☎ 0332 917451

Hotel du Lac (€)
Elegantly situated, this small and well-kept hotel has an excellent restaurant.
✉ Viale Ungheria 19, 21037 Ponte Tresa ☎ 0332 550308/550463

Villa Principe Leopoldo (€€€)
A distinguished villa in hillside gardens, this lush hideaway has rooms overlooking the lake and mountains. A bit out of the way, but the hotel's van can take you down to central Lugano.
✉ Via Montalbano 5, Lugano ☎ 091 985 88 55; www.leopoldohotel.com

VARESE
City Hotel (€€)
A city hotel within reach of the western lakes. Near the heart of Varese and with parking and access to public transport. No restaurant but good choices nearby.
✉ Via Medaglie d'Oro 35, 21100 Varese ☎ 0332 281304; www.cityhotelvarese.com

RESTAURANTS

LAKE ORTA
Sacro Monte (€€)
Worth a visit for the setting and the house speciality desserts alone. Beautiful building, beautifully positioned. Reserve ahead.
✉ Via Sacro Monte 5, Orta San Giúlio ☎ 0322 90220 ⏰ Daily lunch and dinner

Trattoria Toscana (€)
Surprisingly inexpensive, considering it's one of the best places on the lake. Specializes in lake fish dishes, but good overall choice.
✉ Via Mazzini 153, Omegna ☎ 0323 62460 ⏰ Thu–Tue lunch and dinner

Villa Crespi (€€€)

One of the most unusual places on the lake, this eccentric 19th-century villa, in parkland, looks like a stage set for *Arabian Nights*. The restaurant has two Michelin stars and serves sophisticated Mediterranean cuisine. The villa is also a small hotel.

✉ Via Fava 8–10 (about 2km/3 miles to the east of Orta San Giúlio) ☎ 0323 911902 ◑ Thu–Tue lunch and dinner, by reservation only

LAKE MAGGIORE

Il Battello del Golfo (€€–€€€)

You can't miss this beautifully restored lake steamer docked at the harbour. The food is as outstanding as the setting.

✉ Lungolago, Feriolo ☎ 0323 28122; www.battellodelgolfo.com ◑ Jul, Aug Wed–Mon dinner; Sep–Jun Wed–Sun dinner

Belvedere (€–€€)

Try ravioli of *luccio* (pike) with lavender, or grilled lamb cutlet *alla scottadito* (pounded until it's thin, then cooked quickly). With reservations they will provide the boat ride to and from the island.

✉ Via di Mezzo, Isola Pescatori ☎ 0323 32292; www.belvedere-isolapescatori.it

Concordia (€)

Popular with the locals, which is usually a good sign.

✉ Piazza Marchetti 7, Laveno ☎ 0332 667380 ◑ Mid-Feb to Dec Tue–Sun lunch and dinner

Dell Gallo (€€)

Interesting place in Feriolo village where the road for the Simplon Pass splits from the lake road. Good cooking and service.

✉ Strasse Nationale Sempione 16, Feriolo ☎ 032 328110 ◑ Daily lunch and dinner

Elvezia (€€)

The best place on Isola Bella. Good menu and cooking, and all in a romantic setting.

✉ Isola Bella ☎ 0323 30043; www.elvezia.it ◑ Daily lunch and dinner

L'Emiliano (€€€)

Excellent cooking in a lovely setting. The specialities are ravioli and lamb.

✉ Corso Italia 50, Stresa ☎ 0323 31396 🕐 Daily lunch and dinner

Il Gabbiano (€)

A moderately priced restaurant with a chef that keys his menu to the season. In autumn look for dishes featuring Alba white truffles and fresh wild mushrooms.

✉ Via Maggio 19, Baveno ☎ 0323 924496; www.ristoranteilgabbiano.info 🕐 Daily lunch and dinner

Grotto Sant' Anna (€€)

Close to Orrido Sant' Anna gorge, the traditional grotto serves local dishes prepared and presented with great care. Try the *tagliolini al tartufo* (truffle).

✉ Via Sant' Anna 30, Cannóbio ☎ 0323 70682 🕐 Daily lunch and dinner

Isolino (€)

The wait for the car ferry from Intra to Laveno is never long. But just in case you have time to spare, this delightful little restaurant provides good cooking at a moderate price.

✉ Piazza San Vittore 3A, Intra ☎ 0323 53897 🕐 Daily lunch and dinner

Milano (€€–€€€)

Stone-ground flour in the freshly made pasta and only fish from Lake Maggiore – that's how fussy the chef is about ingredients, and it shows in dishes such as marinated wild boar or duck in Cognac.

✉ Corso Zanitello 2, Pallanza ☎ 0323 556816 🕐 Wed–Sun lunch and dinner, Mon lunch

L'Osteria (€€)

A wine bar in vaulted cellars, where an outstanding chef serves dishes such as veal in Madeira and pork medallions with porcini – and bakes delectable tarts.

✉ Via Verdi 5, Feriolo di Baveno ☎ 0323 280482 🕐 Wed–Mon lunch and dinner

Osteria degli Amici (€–€€)

Dine in a garden in the historical centre, on tagliatelle served with a truffle cream sauce and Nodino di Vitello, a small veal steak with butter and sage. Pizza is baked in a wood oven.

✉ Via A M Bolongaro 33, Stresa ✉ 0323 30453 ⏰ Daily lunch and dinner

Piemontese (€€)

Offers genuine Piedmontian cuisine in a very pleasant building.

✉ Via Mazzini 25, Stresa ☎ 0323 330235 ⏰ Tue–Sun lunch and dinner. Closed Sun off-season

La Quartina (€€)

Away from Lake Maggiore, in a village at the head of a smaller lake. Very picturesque: in summer meals are served on the terrace overlooking the lake. Excellent menu, with some local dishes.

✉ Via Pallanza 20, Mergozzo ☎ 0323 80118; www.laquartina.com ⏰ Jun–Aug daily lunch and dinner; Sep–May Tue–Sun lunch and dinner

Lo Scalo (€€€)

The menu offers superb choice but the fish dishes are the restaurant's speciality. Enjoy alfresco in the lakeside garden.

✉ Piazza Vittorio Emanuele II 32, Cannóbio ☎ 0323 71480 ⏰ Wed–Sun dinner. Additional lunch sitting in August

Il Torchio (€€)

Quite small, so you may need to make reservations, but it is worth the effort.

✉ Via Manzoni 20, Pallanza ☎ 0323 503352 ⏰ Thu–Tue lunch and dinner

Trattoria Tre Re (€€)

Rustic pizzeria that also serves local pasta specialities and lake fish.

✉ Via Manzoni 29, Luino ☎ 0332 531147 ⏰ Tue–Sun lunch and dinner

LAKE LUGANO
Locanda del Ghitello (€€)

There's nothing rustic about this *locanda* near the Valle di Muggio except its setting. Artistic presentations vie for attention with the flavours in dishes such as a terrine of foie gras and figs or rabbit braised with pancetta and sage.

✉ Morbio Inferiore ☎ 091 6822061; www.locandadelghitello.ch 🕐 Mon, Thu, Fri lunch and dinner, Tue, Wed lunch, Sat dinner. Reserve ahead

Motto del Gallo (€€€)

From the venison and partridge terrine to the coconut bavarian with fig and hazelnut *gelato*, it's a class act.

✉ Via Bicentenario 16, Taverne (Lugano) ☎ 091 9452871; www.mottodelgallo.ch 🕐 Wed–Sat lunch and dinner, Tue dinner

Villa Sassa (€€€)

The view over Lugano is as glittering as the menu at this restaurant, which is part of a hotel. Dishes might include a tartare of tuna with guacamole or a gratin of fresh figs in Port with pistachio ice cream.

✉ Via Tesserete 10, Lugano ☎ 091 911 4111; www.villasassa.ch 🕐 Daily lunch and dinner

ENTERTAINMENT

Fico d'India

Disco pub with a regular cabaret. On Friday the music is live.

✉ Via Papa Innocenzon 37, Vedano Olona ☎ 0332 400125

Kelly Green

An interesting place that has retained its position as the best of local nightlife spots. The venue combines indoor and outdoor (garden) disco. Dance under the stars until 4am, but only on weekends.

✉ Via Lungolago Gramsci 33, Omegna ☎ 0323 862917

Pardo Bar

Behind the Hotel Angelo at the end of Piazza Grande. During the day this is an expensive internet café, but at night it is the noisiest place in town. The music is not live, but certainly insistent. Great range of drinks.

✉ Via della Motta 3, Locarno ☎ 091 7522123

Lake Como, Bergamo and the Valleys

Lago di Como

Bergamo

Once a glacier filled the valleys that now carry the Adda and Mera rivers. It flowed south, bumping against the vast triangle of rock that now underlies the High Brianza, its tip at the Punta Spartivento (near Bellágio).

The rock of the triangle was hard, splitting the glacier and deepening two valleys to create a lake that is an inverted Y, the points of its arms at Como and Lecco. Interestingly, the Lecco arm lies a little higher than the Como arm so that the lake flows through the Adda, which flows past Lecco. There is no outlet on the Como arm and when rain increases the lake's volume beyond that which can be easily taken by the Adda the lake overflows, occasionally flooding Piazza Cavour, the lakeside square in Como.

Lake Como

This is the most elegant of the lakes. Renowned for its gentle winter climate, Lake Como became the favourite destination of Europe's nobility and super-rich during the 19th century. Some built villas, sumptious buildings set among gardens, lovingly landscaped with plants that thrived in an ideal climate of abundant sun, water and gentle winters. These villas and gardens set a tone that has never been eroded by mass tourism, making Lake Como a place for those who value peace and tranquillity. Perhaps the best way to appreciate the lake is from the many boats that connect its towns daily.

✚ 5B 🚢 800 551801; www.navigazionelaghi.it

ARGEGNO

Argegno is a pretty town, best seen from the road that descends from the Intelvi villages (➤ 62–63), when the red-tiled roofs of the houses stand out against the wooded valley of the Telo river and the lake. The view from the lake front is superb, with a long arm of the lake in both directions and, northwards, the mountains above Varenna, snow-capped in winter. To make the best of the view, go just a little out of town to the north and take the *funivia* to Pigra, well known not only for its scenic views but also for the profusion of wild flowers that grow near the top station.

✚ 5C ✉ On Lake Como's western shore 🍴 La Griglia (€), 1 Fraz Sant'Anna; 031 821147; www.lagriglia.it 🚌 Regular buses from Como 🚢 Regular lake steamers

BELLÁGIO

Best places to see, ➤ 36–37.

BELLANO

On the lake front of Bellano there are memorials to the 19th-century writer Tommaso Grossi and the 17th-century scientist Sigismondo Boldoni. Neither of the pair is very well known outside

Italy, but Bellano is proud of its famous sons. It is also proud of the fact that it was another member of the Boldoni family, Pietro, who introduced the silk industry to Como.

The town's old quarter is very attractive, with a fine church, but most visitors come to see the *orrido,* the gorge of the Pioverna stream. In spring melting snow swells the stream and over the centuries the extra volume has cut a deep, narrow and wildly convoluted gorge through the rocks above the town. Walkways allow you to explore the gorge. When the stream level is high the spray and constant hammering of the water make it an exciting journey.

✚ 5B ✉ On Lake Como's eastern shore 🍴 La Darsena (€€), Via Alberto 8; 0341 810317 🚌 Regular buses along the eastern shore from Lecco 🚢 Regular lake steamers

CADENÁBBÍA

Although most of Como's shore enjoys a mild climate, the western towns between Ossuccio and Cadenábbía get even more winter sunlight. As a result, the area, known as the Tremezzina, has a heavier concentration of villas and gardens. Most famous of these is Villa Carlotta (▶ 54–55). A good way to see these lakeside villas

and to glimpse into some of the private gardens is by walking the newly designated Lake Como Greenway. The walking route hugs the shore from the northern end of Cadenábbía past Tremezzo, then turns inland through Mezzegra, returning to the shore again above Lenno. Maps of the route are posted at all the public boat landings, making it easy to walk sections and return by boat.

Verdi stayed in a villa in Cadenábbía while finishing his score for *La Traviata*. The village is a terminus for Como's main car ferry, linking Cadenábbía with Bellágio and Varenna.

✚ 5B ✉ On Lake Como's western shore 🍴 La Marianna (€€), Via Regina 57, Cadenábbía; 0344 43095; www.la-marianna.com 🚌 Regular buses along the lake's western shore ⛴ Regular lake steamers and car ferries link to Varenna and Bellágio

CERNOBBIO

Passengers alighting from the lake steamer at Cernobbio are welcomed by a wide piazza filled with cafés and backed by the warren of narrow streets of the old town. By contrast, on the main street at the southern edge of the old town is one of the landmark buildings of the 20th-century Italian Rationalist era, Casa Cattaneo. A few streets farther south is the astonishing Villa Bernasconi, a riot of art nouveau. North of the centre, visible only from a boat or to its guests, is the lake's most sumptuous hotel, Villa d'Este. Built as a cardinal's palace in the 16th century, it has elaborate gardens, with a waterfall and castellated lookouts, which are sometimes open to the public. North of Cernobbio, follow signs to Monte Bisbino, where a road climbs to the top for spectacular views.

✚ 4C ✉ On Lake Como's western shore 🍴 Hostaria Ristorante (€€), Via Garibaldi 3; 031 513078 🚌 Infrequent buses along the western shore from Como ⛴ Regular lake steamers

COMO

Como occupies an ancient site that has been inhabited since at least the Bronze Age. During the Roman period Julius Caesar himself brought 5,000 Greeks to settle in the town, the start of its rise to prosperity. After the fall of Rome, Como was the home of the Maestri Comacina, a group of architects, builders and sculptors whose work is still admired today throughout northern Italy. The disastrous Ten Years War (1118–1127) with Milan ruined the town, but it recovered and became noted for its wool and silk industries. Today Como is still the heart of Italian silk production.

✚ 4C

Broletto

Piazza Duomo lies just a few steps inland from Piazza Cavour and the lake. As you enter the square, the first building on your left is the Broletto, the 13th-century town hall. It has an arcaded ground floor with triple-arched windows above, and is attached to a tall campanile.

✉ Piazza Duomo

Duomo

Dominating Piazza Duomo is the west façade of the cathedral, a masterpiece of Gothic architecture with statues peering out from its niches. Two of the statues are not of the usual saints but of the Romans Pliny the Elder and Younger. The façade dates from the 15th century, but the Duomo took many years to complete and includes a range of styles that show the transition from medieval Gothic to Renaissance. The dome was added only in the 18th century. The oldest section of the building was the work of the Rodari brothers and it was they who carved the exquisite south door and the Porta della Rana, the Frog door, on the north side, so called because there is a frog carved on one pillar. Inside, the Duomo has a fine rose window, good stone carving and paintings by Bernardino Luini.

✉ Piazza Duomo ☎ 031 256244

🍴 L'Imbarcadero (€€€), Piazza Cavour 20; 031 269444. La Colonne (€€), Piazza Mazzini 12; 031 266166

Museo Civico

An outstanding museum filling two former palaces with local Neolithic and Bronze-Age artifacts, Roman relics, medieval stone carving and more modern exhibits on Garibaldi.

✉ Via Vittorio Emanuele ☎ 031 271343 🕐 Tue–Sat 9:30–12:30, 2–5, Sun 10–1 💰 Inexpensive

Porta Vittoria

At the far end of the old town from the lake is a tall, sturdy tower built in the 12th century to protect one of the gates through the old wall. During the wars of the Risorgimento Garibaldi defeated an Austrian army under Marshall Urban at nearby San Fermo and marched in triumph through Porta Vittoria.

✉ Via Cantú/Piazza Vittoria

Sant'Abbondio and San Carpoforo

These two fine basilicas, both the work of the Maestri Comacina, are named after early Christians who preached in the area. With its severe façade and twin towers, Sant'Abbondio is recognized as one of the great masterpieces of the Lombard Romanesque style. Inside, superb 14th-century frescoes illustrate the life of Christ.

San Carpoforo is thought to occupy the site of a Roman temple to Mercury, but has a Christian tradition that is at least 1,500 years old. The exterior is similar to that of Sant'Abbondio, but inside it is a complete contrast, with elegant steps and unfrescoed walls.

Sant'Abbondio ✉ Via Sant'Abbondio
San Carpoforo ✉ Via Brenta

San Fedele

San Fedele is probably the finest of Como's trio of churches built by the Maestri Comacina. This wonderful building has breathtaking frescoes dating from the 14th to the 16th centuries. Take time, however, to enjoy its exterior with a stroll around the square.

✉ Piazza San Fedele

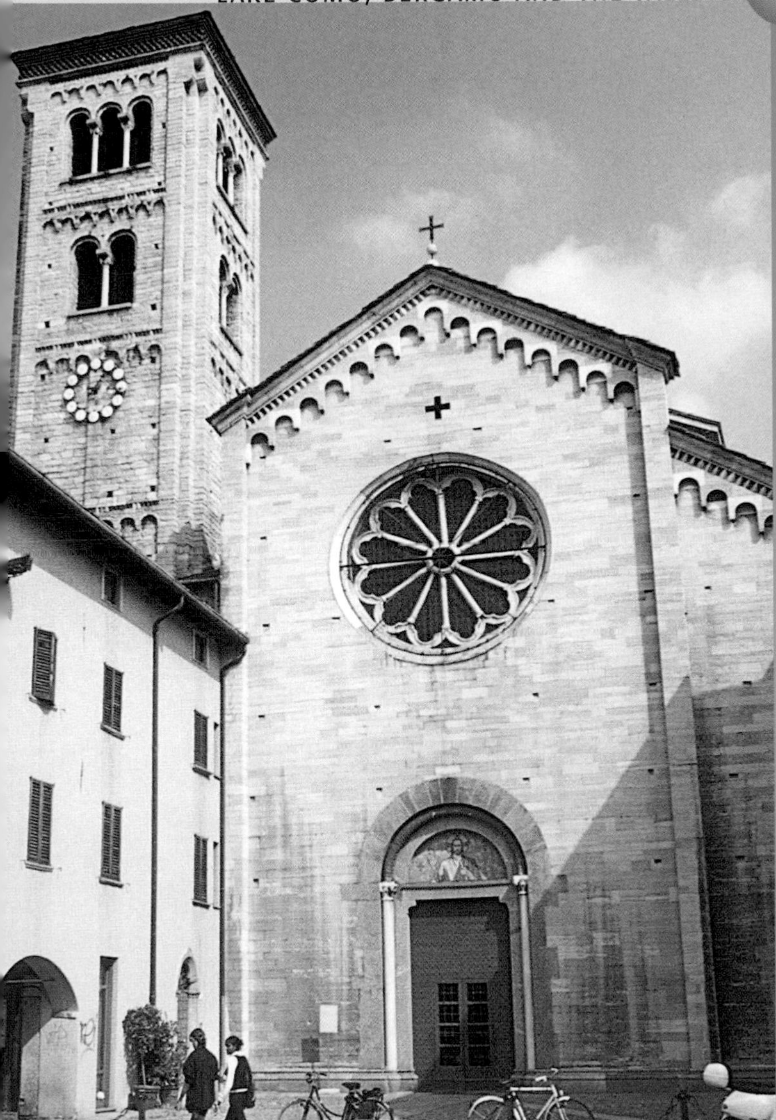

GRAVEDONA

Gravedona is a good base for exploring the northern section of Lake Como's western shore. In medieval times the town was the senior partner of the Tre Pievi – the Three Parishes, the other two being Dongo and Sorico – which maintained its independence from the city states to the south. The Tre Pievi occasionally supplemented trade with piracy, using a ship with a golden crucifix attached to the prow, which the villagers claimed made it invincible. Once the ship attacked and defeated a treasure ship of the Emperor Frederick I (the feared Barbarossa – 'Red Beard'). The Emperor was outraged, but the gold was to support his campaign against the Lombard League and after his defeat at the battle of Legnano in 1176 he was forced to make concessions in the Treaty of Constance in 1183. Some of those concessions were to the Tre Pievi.

Gravedona has some fine buildings.

The town council now occupies the 'Villa of Delights' of Cardinal Tolomeo Gallio (who also owned Villa d'Este at Cernobbio ➤ 133). Away from the town centre, overlooking Lake Como, is Santa Maria del Tiglio. Built in the 12th century, on the foundations of a 5th-century baptistery dedicated to St John the Baptist, the Romanesque church contains outstanding fresco cycles from the 14th and 15th centuries. The font and part of the mosaic floor survive from the original baptistery; the altar is from the Romanesque era. Dongo, a little way south of Gravedona, had entered history as the site of Mussolini's capture.

The northwestern section of Lake Como is famous for its reliable winds and has become a favourite with sailors and water sports enthusiasts. Pianello del Lario, south of Gravedona, is the home of the lake's most important sailing club, while to the north, the pretty village of Domaso is the best place on Lake Como for windsurfing.

✚ 5B ⁉️ Lauro (€), Via Tagliaferri 17, Gravedona; 034 485255 🚌 Regular buses along the western shore 🚢 Regular lake steamers

LECCO

There is a good deal of rivalry between Lecco and Como. The cities are about equal in size, and while Como is more historically interesting (and, most unbiased observers would maintain, more elegant), Lecco is without doubt more dramatically located, beside the lake's only outflow river and below the steep cliffs of Monte Coltignone to the northwest, and the Resegone to the east. Though the Como arm of the lake and its single northern reach are part of Lake Como, it would be a brave person who would not refer to the eastern arm as Lake Lecco when staying in the town.

Piani d'Erna is a popular walking area beneath the Resegone; you get there by a cable car from Versasio above the town, which offers a splendid view of Lecco and the lake.

The town lies on the lake's eastern shore and is reached from the west by two bridges that span the Adda. The farthest of these from the lake is Ponte Visconti, built on the orders of Azzone Visconti in 1336. The original bridge had drawbridge sections at each end. When it was renovated to look as it had when originally built, its 11 arches were maintained, but plans stopped short of reproducing the drawbridges. In Piazza XX Septembre, the Torre Visconti is another reminder of Milanese influence. A market has been held in the square below the tower since at least 1149. Elsewhere, there is a fine statue of Lecco's famous writer, Alessandro Manzoni (1785–1873); his childhood home is now a **museum** with a collection of memorabilia. The town's tourist office has a leaflet identifying places mentioned in Manzoni's book *The Betrothed*. Most of the sites are actually in Olate, a village above and east of the town. To the north of Villa Manzoni is **Palazzo Belgioioso,** a 17th-century mansion that now houses the town's museum.

✚ 6C ⊠ At the southern tip of Lake Como's eastern arm 🚌 Regular buses from Como 🚢 Regular lake steamers 🍴 Cermenati (€€), Corso Matteotti 71; 0341 283017

Manzoni Museum

⊠ Via Guonella 5 ☎ 0341 481249; www.museilecco.org 🕓 Tue–Sun 9:30–2 💰 Moderate

Palazzo Belgioioso

⊠ Corso Matteotti 32 ☎ 0341 481248; www.museilecco.org 🕓 Tue–Sun 9:30–2 💰 Moderate 🚌 Regular buses from Como

MENÁGGIO

Menággio's position, halfway along the western shore of Lake Como, where an easy route links the Como valley to the Lugano valley and Switzerland, means that the town has always been an important trading centre. As always, trade brings traffic, but away from this the town is well worth the visit. During the Ten Years War of the 12th century, Menággio chose the wrong side and was destroyed. It was a mistake the townsfolk made again on several occasions in medieval times; they also picked fights with the Spanish and the Austrians during their periods of dominance.

The town has a very good beach – something of a rarity on Lake Como – and one of the most romantically sited golf courses in Italy. It is also a good base for exploring both the Val Menággio and the hills to the northwest. The Val Menággio road passes the little lake of Piano, once part of Lake Lugano but separated from it by a landslide. The lake is now part of a nature reserve.

From Menággio the minor road to Pièsio and Breglia passes through Loveno, a village that is almost unchanged since early medieval times. From Breglia, a good walk climbs Monte Grona, with views of both Lake Como and Lake Lugano, while a longer

walk follows the upper parts of Valle Sanagra to Monte Bregagno and an even wider panorama.

✚ 5B 🍴 Osteria Il Pozzo (€€), Piazza Garibaldi; 0344 32333 🚌 Regular buses from Como and Porlezza 🚢 Regular lake steamers; car ferries from Varenna/Bellagio

PIONA

At the northern end of Lake Como's eastern shore, two spits of land almost touch, creating the sheltered bay of Laghetto di Piona, the little Piona lake. At the point of the western headland sits the **Abbey of Piona**. It is likely that this site was an ancient and holy one even before the Christian era, and there was certainly a Christian church before the abbey was founded by the Cluniac monks in 1138. Early in the 20th century the abbey was taken over by Cistercians. The monks distil liqueurs, including Gocce Imperiali, which has a reputation for being really potent. Parts of the abbey are open to visitors. The church is the oldest section but the mid-13th-century cloisters, a lovely mix of Gothic and Renaissance styles, are the most interesting. Outside the abbey the small garden offers wonderful views across the lake to Gravedona.

North of Lake Piona is Colico, built at the edge of the marshland of Piano di Spagna, famous for its wildlife and migrating birds. Close to the Valtellina, the valley of the Adda and the Spluga Pass, the town was by turns prosperous on trade and subject to attacks by bandits. South of the abbey, Corenno Plinio is a pretty village named after Pliny the Elder, who loved this section of the lake. Just beyond is Dervio, filling a rounded headland where the lake is at its narrowest. The strategic importance of this is reflected in the sparse ruins of medieval fortifications.

✚ 6B ✉ At the northern end of Lake Como's eastern shore 🍴 Albergo Ristorante Belvedere (€€), Via Olgiasca 53, Colico; 0341 940330 🚢 Regular lake steamers from Colico

Piona Abbey

☎ 0341 940331 🕐 Daily 9–12, 2–6 🎫 Free

SALA COMACINA AND ISOLA COMACINA

A place of refuge and a hermitage for saints, Lake Como's only island, just off Sala Comacina's pretty little harbour, has had a tumultuous history. Inhabited at least since Roman times, the island already had several churches when wealthy Christians fled here from Atilla the Hun. In the sixth century, when Lombards conquered northern Italy, the Byzantine governor escaped to Isola Comacina, and later the Lombards' own king hid here. Holy Roman Emperor Frederick Barbarossa found refuge in the 12th century.

At least three saints had hermitages here, and St Abonde founded a basilica whose low walls and stone floors remain beside the later baroque Oratorio, still standing. Take a boat from Sala Comacina to the island and follow the trail uphill to the foundations of Santa Maria col Portico among the olive trees, then continue to the ruined medieval basilica, the oratorio and behind it a paleo-Christian baptistry with fifth-century mosaics and eighth-century frescoes. The island is a good place to take a picnic lunch to eat among the stones.

✚ 5B ✉ Sala Comacina

VARENNA

The houses of Varenna have been built on a steep hill on top of which sit the ruins of a castle (Castello Vezio), which was the last home of Theodolinda, a seventh-century Lombard queen. The castle controlled the lake at the point where it divides and, situated on its outcrop of the Grigna, was virtually impregnable. The castle gave the village that grew up around it a certain prosperity, which was enhanced when the survivors of Como's destruction of Isola Comacina made their homes here and opened a quarry for the black marble found in outcrops nearby. The marble quarry kept the town prosperous for many years. By contrast, the product of a later son of the town did nothing for the local economy. G B Pirelli was born in Varenna, but his tyre empire did not include a Varenna factory. The Pirelli calendars were never produced here either.

Besides the array of fine old houses, Varenna has two superb villas. Villa Cipressi (villa open only to guests; gardens open to the public) has terraced gardens going down to the lake edge and lovely views across the water. Neighbouring **Villa Monastero** is even more impressive, both for its building and its gardens. The villa was constructed in 1208 for Cistercian nuns but in the 16th century the sisters acquired a reputation for conduct distinctly unchaste and the convent was closed on the orders of San Carlo Borromeo. The villa, beautifully maintained and furnished, is now

used as a summer school for the sciences. It is a beautiful building with a stone staircase rising from the lake, lovely arched windows and an arcaded terrace. The terraced grounds are equally attractive, with fine shrubbery and masses of citrus trees.

Back in the village, birdwatchers will want to visit the **ornithological museum,** where all the species that have been seen on the lake are displayed.

⊞ 5B ⊠ On Lake Como's eastern shore 🍴 Vecchia Varenna (€€), Contrada Scoscesa 10; 0341 830793 🚌 Regular buses from Lecco ⛴ Regular lake steamers and car ferries

Villa Monastero
⊠ Viale G Polvani ☎ 0341 295450; www.villamonastero.eu 🕐 Mar to mid-Jun, Sep, Oct Sat, Sun, holidays 9–1, 2–6; mid-Jun to Aug Fri 2–7, Sat, Sun, holidays 9–7

Museo Civico Ornitologico
⊠ Via Corrado Venini 6 ☎ 0341 830119 🕐 Mar–May, Oct, Nov Sun 10–12; Jun–Sep Wed, Thu, Sat 3–6, Sun 10–12 ✋ Inexpensive

VILLA BALBIANELLO
The setting for a villa doesn't get much better than this. The baroque Villa Balbianello, built by Cardinal Durini in the 1700s, stands at the very tip of a steep peninsula almost entirely surrounded by Lake Como. All around it, cascading down the steep slopes to the water, are perfectly manicured gardens with terraces bounded by balustrades with statuary. Giant trees, flowering shrubs, statues and urns of flowers are placed to frame views of the lake, and the walkways are bordered in a succession of colourful flower beds. From late April through mid-June azaleas and rhododendrons are in full bloom.

The best views of the villa and grounds are from the passing lake steamers and from the small water taxis that take visitors from Lenno, but those are only passing glimpses and do not replace a visit to see the gardens and the views from the villa. Boats leave Lenno during the garden's opening hours, or you can visit the gardens on foot by a 2km (1-mile) walking path from Lenno (the gate for this path is open only on Tuesday, Saturday, Sunday and holidays).

✚ 5B ✉ Lenno ☎ 0344 56110 ⚙ Mid-Mar to mid-Nov Tue, Thu–Sun 10–6 ✋ Moderate (gardens only)

VILLA CARLOTTA
Best places to see, ➤ 54–55.

Bergamo and the Valleys

The relatively unknown city of Bergamo has a
long history and a beautifully preserved
medieval heart. North of Bergamo, two valleys,
each with numerous branches, head back
towards the mountains that form the southern
ridge of the Valtellina.

BERGAMO

Bergamo is two cities, the modern lower one
and the medieval upper one (Città Alta). Though
the main attractions are concentrated in the
Città Alta, visitors should not ignore the lower
city. The monument to Bergamo-born composer
Donizetti (1797–1848) is in Piazza Cavour,
while the theatre named after him is on the
Sentierone, which links Piazza Cavour to Piazza
Vittorio Veneto. The **composer's birthplace** and
a **museum** to him can be visited in the Upper
City. The lower city has two fine churches: San
Bartolomeo, with frescoes by Lorenzo Lotto,
and Sant'Alessandro in Colonna. The column
outside the latter church marks the reputed spot
where the saint was martyred in AD297. On the
street to the Upper City is the Accademia
Carrara; if it is still closed for renovations, you
can see part of its collection in the Palazzo della
Ragione, in Piazza Vecchia.

The focus in the Upper City is the Piazza
Vecchia (➤ 48–49), but there is much else to
see. In Piazza del Duomo stands the cathedral,
dating from the mid-15th century (though the
dome and façade are 19th century). Beside
the cathedral is the basilica of **Santa Maria**

Maggiore, a 12th-century building with a superb porch in red and white marble and a sumptuous interior. Built into the side of the basilica is the **Colleoni Chapel,** by Bartolomeo Colleoni, a *condottiere* (mercenary soldier) who twice captained Venetian forces against Milan and twice led the Milanese against Venice, growing rich in the process. Colleoni built the chapel as his mausoleum and died in 1476 just after it was finished. Behind the Duomo is the 9th-century Tempietto di Santa Croce, and a passageway through the entry hall to the diocese offices, with excellent 13th-century frescoes. ✚ 7D

Museo Donizettiano

✉ 9 Via Arena, Upper City ☎ 035 399269; http://fondazione.bergamoestoria.it 🕐 Jun–Sep Tue–Sun 9:30–1, 2–5:30 💵 Inexpensive

Basilica of Santa Maria Maggiore

✉ Piazza del Duomo ☎ 035 223327/246855 🕐 Daily 9–12:30, 2–6:30 (4:30 Nov–Feb) 💵 Free

Colleoni Chapel

✉ Piazza del Duomo ☎ 035 210061 🕐 Mar–Oct daily 9–12:30, 2–6:30; Nov–Feb 9–12:30, 2–4:30 💵 Free

VAL BREMBANA

Brembana is the westerly of the two valleys. The Brembo River's geography meant that until the 17th century only two difficult passes allowed entry into the valley, the isolation allowing the local people to evolve a rich folklore, including their own dialect and architectural style. At Almenno San Bartolomeo, the **Museo del Falegname** is devoted to the local craft of woodworking. At Sedrina a picturesque series of bridges crosses the river. The rock here is limestone and has been eaten away by rain and river water to form caves. One, the **Grotte delle Meraviglie,** can be visited. Farther on there is a good **museum of the valley** in Zogno. San Pellegrino Terme is the best-known village in the valley. Once one of the leading spas in Lombardy, it is now famous for its mineral water, which can be found in almost every town in Italy. Beyond San Pellegrino there are enough small villages and remote side valleys to keep the visitor entertained for several days. At the head of the valley, Foppolo is the best-developed ski resort in the area.

✚ 7C

Museo del Falegname

✉ Via Papa Giovanni XXIII, Almenno San Bartolomeo

☎ 035 544411; www.tinosana.com/museo

🕐 Sep–Jun Sat 3–6, Sun 9:30–12, 3–6

✋ Inexpensive 🍴 Palanca (€), Via Dogana 15; 035 640800

Grotte delle Meraviglie

✉ Sedrina ☎ 0345 91044/55007 🕐 May–Sep some Sun 2:30–6. Check dates with local tourist office

✋ Inexpensive

Museo della Valle
✉ Via Mazzini 3, Zogno ☎ 0345 91473;
www.museodellavalle.com 🕐 Tue–Sun
9–12, 2–5 ✋ Inexpensive

VAL SERIANA
The lower reaches of the Serio river valley are industrialized, but the upper valley remains unspoiled. Abbazia is named after its 12th-century Cistercian abbey, a delightful building. Farther on is Gandino, with a medieval gateway and a fine 15th-century basilica with a baroque interior. From the village a chairlift takes visitors to a plateau that is a ski resort in winter and offers good walking in summer. Farther on is Vertova, where the church is surrounded by an arcade that makes it look like a hen protecting her chicks. There is an even more impressive church at Clusone. The Oratorio dei Disciplini has frescoes that include a 'Dance of Death', people and skeletons hand in hand. The final village in the valley is Valbondione, from which a walk leads to the Cascata del Serio, reputedly Europe's highest waterfall at 315m (1,033ft). Sadly the stream that feeds it is now diverted into a hydroelectric station, the waterfall only being 'turned on' during certain summer weekends.
✚ 8C

HOTELS

LAKE COMO

Alberi (€–€€)

Ideally located for exploring Lecco, the Grigna mountains and the Lecco arm of the lake. Good facilities. No restaurant but close to some very good ones.

✉ Lungo Lario Isonzo 4, 23900 Lecco ☎ 0341 350992; www.hotelalberi.lecco.it

Barchetta (€€€)

The best location, right at the edge of the main square and facing the lake. Comfortable modern decor and a very good restaurant.

✉ Piazza Cavour 1, 22100 Como ☎ 031 3221; www.hotelbarchetta.it

Centrale (€€)

In the heart of town, just a few steps away from the lake steamer quay. Its air-conditioned rooms have internet access. Excellent restaurant, with an alfresco option in the garden in summer.

✉ Via Regina 39, 22012 Cernobbio ☎ 031 511411

Grand Hotel Tremezzo (€€€)

Superb hotel, one of the oldest on the lake and built in grand style with gardens to match. Some rooms share balconies overlooking the lake. Excellent restaurant.

✉ Via Regina 8, 22019 Tremezzo ☎ 0344 42491; www.grandhoteltremezzo.com ⏲ Mar–Nov

Grand Hotel Victoria (€€€)

Beautiful old building in delightful grounds. Very good French restaurant with alfresco option.

✉ Lungolago Castelli 7/11, 22017 Menággio ☎ 0344 32003; www.centrohotelslakecomo.com

Grand Hotel Villa d'Este (€€€)

With a claim to being the finest hotel on the lakes, and one of the best in Italy, the building is almost a museum, filled with fine art.

✉ Via Regina 40, 22012 Cernobbio ☎ 031 3481; www.villadeste.it

Grand Hotel Villa Serbelloni (€€€)

Magnificent and magnificently located villa, now a world-class hotel with a superb restaurant and luxury spa.

✉ Via Roma 1, 22021 Bellágio ☎ 031 950216; www.villaserbelloni.it
🕐 Easter–Oct

Royal Victoria (€€)

Close to the car ferry so very good for those planning to travel around the lake. Queen Victoria stayed here. Fine restaurant.

✉ Piazza San Giorgio 5, 23829 Varenna ☎ 0341 815111;
www.royalvictoria.com

BERGAMO
Arli (€€)

Close to the *funivia* for the Città Alta and the lower city's shopping area. Good facilities. No restaurant, but near many excellent ones.

✉ Largo Porta Nuovo 12, 24121 Bergamo (lower city) ☎ 035 222077

Cappello d'Oro (€€€)

Just a short walk from the lower station of the *funivia* to the Upper City. Very well appointed with a good restaurant.

✉ Viale Papa Giovanni XXIII 12, 24121 Bergamo (lower city) ☎ 035 232503

Hotel Bigio (€€)

In town and close to the river, the Bigio has its own good dining room and private gardens.

✉ Viale Papa Giovanni XXII 60, San Pellegrino ☎ 0345 21058/21687;
www.bigio.info

RESTAURANTS

COMO
Cucina di Elsa (€–€€)

Tired of pasta? Try Elsa's savoury shrimp on a bed of julienned courgette (zucchini), one of many tempting combinations on the menu.

✉ Via Carcano Paolo 11, Como ☎ 031 267523; www.lacucinadielsa.com
🕐 Mon–Sat 9–3:30, 6:30–12

Da Pietro (€€)

Nicely positioned on the cathedral square. Good cooking and a pleasant atmosphere.

✉ Piazza Duomo 16, Como ☎ 031 264005 ⏰ Tue–Sun lunch and dinner

Don Lisander (€€)

Basement restaurant/pizzeria on the lake-front road. Good choice and ambiance.

✉ Lungo Lario Trento 19, Como ☎ 031 261417 ⏰ Daily lunch and dinner

Hosterietta (€€)

In the pedestrianized square a little way from Piazza Cavour, this restaurant specializes in risotto; order any with truffles.

✉ Piazza Volta 57, Como ☎ 031 241516 ⏰ Tue–Sun lunch and dinner

Imbarcadero (€€€)

Part of the Hotel Metropole Suisse on the main square. Superb menu and cooking and the option of eating on the square with lake views. Try the lake perch with rice.

✉ Piazza Cavour 20, Como ☎ 031 277341 ⏰ Daily lunch and dinner

Il Solito Posto (€€–€€€)

In the heart of the old town, with a garden for summer dining. Very good menu, with exceptional meat dishes and carpaccio.

✉ Via Lambertenghi 9, Como ☎ 031 271352 ⏰ Tue–Sun lunch and dinner

LAKE COMO
Barchetta (€€)

The extensive menu here is well-executed; look for specials such as rabbit with polenta, and the outstanding autumn truffle menu.

✉ Piazza Roma 2, Argegno ☎ 031 821105; www.ristorantebarchetta.it
⏰ Wed–Mon lunch and dinner

Bilacus (€€)

Away from the lake front and up a steep side street. Very pleasant rooftop terrace and beautifully prepared and presented food.

✉ 32 Via Serbelloni 32, Bellágio ☎ 031 950480 ⏰ Daily lunch and dinner

Da Mario (€)

Family-run restaurant – and it shows in the friendly atmosphere.
Reasonable prices and a good menu stocked with local food.

✉ Via Regina, Domaso ☎ 0344 96309 ⏰ Tue–Sun lunch and dinner

La Darsena (€€)

One of the best places on this part of the lake. Good atmosphere
and excellent food.

✉ Via Alberto 8, Bellano ☎ 0341 810317 ⏰ Daily lunch and dinner

La Griglia (€)

Inexpensive and very good. Well-sited and with an alfresco option.

✉ On the road from Argegno to Schignano/Intelvi ☎ 031 821147
⏰ Wed–Mon dinner

La Laconda dell'Isola Comacina (€€)

Romantically located on Lake Como's island. The same fixed, five-
course menu has been served since 1947.

✉ Isola Comacina ☎ 0344 56755/55083; www.comacina.it ⏰ Jun–Sep
daily lunch and dinner; Mar–May, Oct Wed–Mon lunch and dinner

Ricciolo (€€)

Almost the entire menu is lake fish, prepared in creative ways.
Enjoy beautiful lake views from the terrace.

✉ Via Provinciale 165, Olcio, a small village north of Mandello del Lario
☎ 0341 732546; www.ristorantericciolo.com ⏰ Jun–Aug daily lunch and
dinner; Sep–May Tue–Sat lunch and dinner

Vecchia Varenna (€€)

Perfect renditions of local dishes. Try the trout stuffed with rice and
chicory or wild boar in a bittersweet sauce.

✉ Via Scoscesa 10, Varenna ☎ 0341 830793; www.vecchiavarenna.it
⏰ Feb–Dec Tue–Sun lunch and dinner

BERGAMO AND THE VALLEYS
Colleoni & dell'Angelo (€€€)

A well-loved Bergamo restaurant, in the Città Alta, serving

excellent local ravioli and other favourites in a fine old home.

✉ Piazza Vecchia 7, Bergamo's Upper City ☎ 035 232596;
www.colleonidellangelo.com ⏰ Daily lunch and dinner

Da Vittorio (€€€)

Beautifully presented and brilliantly prepared dishes using local
ingredients, but very, very pricey.

✉ Viale Papa Giovanni XXIII 21, Bergamo ☎ 035 218060;
www.davittorio.com ⏰ Daily lunch and dinner

Taverna Valtellinese (€€)

Situated in Bergamo's lower city. Serves a range of typical dishes
from the Valtellina.

✉ Via Tiraboschi 57, Bergamo ☎ 035 243331 ⏰ Tue–Sun lunch and dinner

ENTERTAINMENT

CLUBS
Lido Menággio

Beach club on the lake with two outdoor pools, a restaurant,
pizzeria and club. Happy hours on Wednesday and Thursday nights.

✉ Via Roma 11, Mennágio ☎ 0344 30645 ⏰ Daily 11:30–2:30, 6:30–12

Il Pappafico

Listen to a DJ or live music while enjoying pizza. Occasionally the
action shifts to a boat.

✉ Viale Geno, Como ☎ 031 303458 ⏰ Thu–Sun from 10pm

Tartaruga

A changing programme every night, everything from R'n'B' to
heavy metal. Frequent live music. Regular Sunday happy hours.

✉ Via Belvedere 122, Villa Guardia ☎ 031 483290 ⏰ Thu–Sun

THEATRE
Gaetano Donizetti Theatre

The theatre promotes classical and contemporary music, including
Donizetti's works, both here and at other local venues.

✉ Piazza Cavour 15, Bergamo ☎ 035 4160601; www.gaetano-donizetti.com

Eastern Lakes and Verona

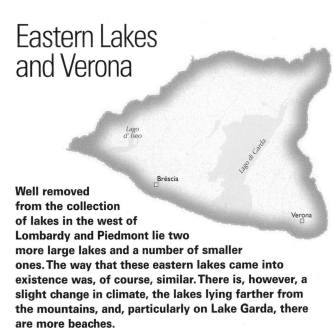

Lago d' Iseo

Lago di Garda

Bréscia

Verona

Well removed from the collection of lakes in the west of Lombardy and Piedmont lie two more large lakes and a number of smaller ones. The way that these eastern lakes came into existence was, of course, similar. There is, however, a slight change in climate, the lakes lying farther from the mountains, and, particularly on Lake Garda, there are more beaches.

Beaches and water sports have made Iseo and Garda centres for sun-seeking tourists. However, this does not mean that there is any shortage of interesting historical sites, beautiful villas and gardens, or walks to be enjoyed on high ridges. There are wonderful cities to visit – Bréscia, with its Roman remains, and lovely Verona, with its Roman, medieval and Renaissance legacies. But there are also more places geared mainly towards entertainment and pleasure.

Bréscia and Lake Idro

Flanked by larger Lakes Como and Garda, and by the better-known cities of Bergamo and Verona, Bréscia and the tree-clad shores of Lake Idro are often overlooked. But the city is rich in Roman relics and the lake a quiet oasis beloved by locals when the larger lakes are crowded with tourists. Connecting the two is the lovely Val Sabbia.

BRÉSCIA

Bréscia is Lombardy's second city, with a population of about 200,000. It stands at the mouth of the Val Trompia, which descends from the pre-Alps of Lombardy's northern border. The city has some of Italy's best Roman remains, and some excellent medieval buildings.

✚ 9E

Colle Cidneo

The oldest part of the city is the hilltop of Colle Cidneo, with its 14th-century Visconti castle. In the castle is the **Risorgimento Museum** and **Arms Museum**. Also on the hilltop are Roman remains and the ruins of a fifth-century church.

Risorgimento Museum

✉ Castello, Colle Cidneo ☎ 030 44176 ⏰ Jun–Sep Tue–Sun 10:30–6; Oct–May Tue–Sun 9:30–5 ✋ Moderate 🍴 La Sosta (€€€), Via San Martino della Battaglia 20; 030 292589; www.lasosta.it

Arms Museum

✉ Castello, Colle Cidneo ☎ 030 293292 ⏰ Jun–Sep Tue–Sun 10:30–6; Oct–May Tue–Sun 9:30–5 ✋ Moderate

Piazza Duomo

There are two cathedrals here, the older one (Duomo Vecchia or Rotonda) dating from the 11th century. It has a severe look, but an unusual circular design, and some remarkable treasures, including a sliver of the True Cross and a Holy Thorn. The newer cathedral is 16th-century baroque, but with a much newer dome. North of the cathedrals is the 13th-century Broletto and the Torre del Popolo, the people's tower.

Piazza Loggia

The Loggia replaced the Broletto as the town hall after it was constructed in the 15th century and still retains that function. The lower floor of the building was designed by Bramante, while the upper floor was by Palladio – a remarkable pedigree. Opposite the Loggia is the Palazzo dell'Orologio, topped by two Venetian figures in distinctly Moorish style. The picturesque older quarter of the city lies close to the piazza.

Via dei Musei

Bréscia's real treasures lie on this street. Here stand the ruins of the **Capitoline Temple** and those of a theatre from the first-century AD, which itself stood at the edge of the forum. Farther along the road is the **Santa Giulia Museo della Città,** in the 16th-century monastery of Santa Giulia, though the site also has the remains of an 8th-century Benedictine nunnery and a 9th-century basilica. The complex houses collections that, until very recently, formed the town's Roman and Christian museums. The Roman treasures include a first-century bronze *Winged Victory* and six bronze busts of second- and third-century emperors. The Christian collection has many priceless items, the best of which include the

Lipsanoteca, a fourth-century ivory reliquary, and the eighth-century jewel-encrusted Cross of Desiderius.

Santa Giulia Museo della Città

✉ Via dei Musei 81 ☎ 030 2977833; www.bresciamusei.com
🕐 Jun–Sep Tue–Sun 10–6; Oct–May 9:30–5:30 ✋ Moderate
🍴 Agora Café (€), Via dei Musei 75; 3358 048861

VAL SABBIA AND LAKE IDRO

East of Bréscia, about halfway between the city and Lake Garda, the N45 road heads north, soon reaching the Chiese river. Geography prevents the Chiese from flowing into the lake, though it seems to want to, bypassing it by just 3km (2 miles) at Salò. From that point, near Tormini, the N237 follows the river closely as it flows through the Val Sabbia near a series of pretty villages. At Sabbio Chiese, the old castle on a large rock outcrop has been transformed into two churches, one on top of the other. Beyond Sabbio Chiese, the valley narrows, the church at Barghe seeming to grow out of the rock. Continue through Vestone, from where roads lead off into the mountains, to reach Lake Idro.

Idro is the highest lake in Lombardy, lying 368m (1,207ft) above sea level. It is 11km (7 miles) long and up to 2km (1.25 miles) wide. In places, especially on the northwestern shore, the mountains fall so steeply into the water that from the opposite shore they seem to rise vertically. Idro, the lake's largest village, lies just off the main road. It is a tourist village and here, and at nearby Crone and Vantone, the campsites fill rapidly in summer. There are more campsites on the western shore, especially near Anfo, where there is a Venetian-built castle on the Rocca d'Anfo. Beyond Anfo a road winds towards the mountains, through Bagolino, a pretty village of narrow streets. Back on the shore road, the visitor reaches Ponte Caffaro, the last village of Val Sabbia.

✚ 10D
🚌 Regular buses from Bréscia and Desenzano del Garda 🍴 Alpino (€€), Crone, Via Lungolago 14, near Idro; 0365 83146

Lake Garda

Lake Garda is best known as a vacation spot, with a string of
campsites around its southern shore. But it has other fine features
too – the historical towns of Sirmione and Malcésine, good
walking areas in Tignale, Tremósine and Monte Baldo, and
excellent restaurants that serve food to enjoy with a glass of local
wine. You can see the mountainous northern end and its
vertiginous towns best from the boats that cross the lake.

🕂 11E 🚢 800 551801; www.navigazionelaghi.it

DESENZANO DEL GARDA

Desenzano is the most important town on the southern lake, with
a railway station on the Milan–Venice line and its own exit from the

A4 *autostrada*. The site has been important for centuries. The Romans built a fort on the Capo la Terra, the highest part of the present town. In medieval times a castle was built on the remains of the Roman works. Roman Desenzano is still evident at **Villa Romana,** the excavated remains of a third- or fourth-century villa. The prize exhibit in the villa is more than 200sq m (240sq yards) of mosaic, depicting hunting scenes and scenes of everyday life. There is a small museum where the best of the excavated finds are displayed. The town also has a **museum** exploring the pre-Roman history of the area. The 16th-century Duomo is also worth visiting to see *The Last Supper* by the Venetian painter Tiepolo.

Desenzano has a very picturesque old harbour, its edges dotted with trees and an array of fine buildings. A large local market is held close to the harbour on Tuesdays. In the evening the harbour is perfect for a romantic stroll.

Just outside Desenzano is the huge medieval fortress of Lonato, on a hilltop with panoramic lake views.

Close to Desenzano, in the village of Padenghe sul Garda, houses have been built within the walls of an old castle, giving it a medieval feel.

➕ 13R 🍴 Caffé Italia (€€), Piazza Malvezzi 19; 030 9141243; www.ristorantecaffeitalia.it 🚌 Regular buses from local towns and villages
🚢 Desenzano is the headquarters and terminus of the Garda lake steamers
🚆 Train station on the line from Milan to Venice

Villa Romana
✉ Via Crocefisso 22 🕓 Apr–Sep Tue–Sun 9–6:30; Nov–Feb 9–4; Mar, Oct 9–5:30 ☎ 030 9143547 ✋ Moderate

Museo Civico Archeologico
✉ Via Anelli 22 🕓 Tue, Fri–Sun 3–7 ☎ 030 9144529 ✋ Free

GARDA

The town named after the lake stands below Monte Garda, a natural fortress topped by the remnants of several castles, the last built by the Scaligeri. Under Scaligeri rule the town's Palazzo dei Capitano was also built, though the name derives from the time of Venetian rule, when the building housed the Serenissima's Captain of the Lake, the local official. A much more impressive building is the Villa Albertini, a romantic, castle-like villa where the treaty was signed that united Piedmont and Lombardy, which many historians date as the start of the Risorgimento. More local history is on display at the **Museo Castello Scaligero** (housed in the remains of yet another Scaligeri castle), in Torri del Benaco, the next village along the eastern shore. This museum also includes several examples of the prehistoric rock engravings found on Monte Luppia and at Punta San Vigilio, both close to Garda. You should visit the Punta itself – though surviving examples of the rock carvings are extremely difficult to find. It is one of the most beautiful places on the lake, with tremendous views across to Manerba and the Salò bay. At the tip is a dignified little church – it has a niche statue that is visible only from the water.

Torri del Benaco, north of Garda, is linked to Maderno by one of Lake Garda's two car ferries (the other connects Malcésine and Limone). South of Garda is Bardolino, famous for its red wine produced from the vineyards covering the hillside above the town.
✚ 16P 🍴 Pizzeria al Padrino (€–€€), Via San Francesco 29; 045 7255379; www.alpadrino.com 🚌 Regular buses along the eastern lake shore
🚢 Regular lake steamers

Museo Castello Scaligero (Tower Museum)
www.museodelcastelloditorridelbenaco.it
✉ Torri del Benaco ☎ 045 6296111 🕐 Jun–Sep daily 9:30–1, 4:30–7.30; Apr, May, Oct daily 9:30–12:30, 2:30–6 🚌 Regular buses along the eastern lake shore

LAZISE
Lazise has another of Garda's Scaligeri castles, almost as impressive as the one at Sirmione, though not as well positioned. The castle is now a private house and cannot be visited. In former times, a chain could be drawn from the castle across the harbour mouth to provide a protective 'wall'. When Lake Garda formed part of the Venetian Republic, a fleet of warships was maintained here, an amazing fact given the small size of the harbour. The Venetians referred to Lazise as the 'Key to Lake Garda' because the fleet controlled the southern lake. Today the harbour is occupied only by a few fishing boats and pleasure craft. Around the harbour are a number of small hotels and cafés that are guaranteed to make any stay in the town a delight. As well as the castle, the town also has sections of its equally impressive arched medieval town wall, complete with fishtail embattlements.
✚ 16Q ✉ On the eastern shore of Lake Garda 🍴 Alla Grotta (€€), Via Francesco Fontana 5; 045 7580035; www.allagrotta.it

LIMONE SUL GARDA

Most people assume the village was named after the lemon trees which, some believe, were grown here for the first time in Europe and made the early village prosperous. Some others claim the lemon story is a legend and that the village is actually named after a son of the god Benacus. The lemon story is certainly supported by the bushes that now grow in profusion, as do orange and mandarin trees. Learn about lemon growing at a restored 18th-century lemon house, **La Limonaia del Castel**, in the upper village. A new road, the Gardesana Occidentale, now speeds visitors along Garda's western shore, bypassing Limone, which has become more of a tourist attraction as a result. The houses of the old quarter, with their balconies and flower boxes, enhance the village's setting below dazzling white cliffs. The church of San Pietro sits in an olive grove on a hill close to the village.

✚ 17J ✉ On the western shore of Lake Garda 🍴 Bellavista (€), Via Marconi 20; 0365 954001; www.bellavistalimone.eu 🚌 Regular buses along the western lake shore 🚢 Regular lake steamers

La Limonaia del Castel
✉ Via Castello ☎ 0365 954008
🕓 Apr–Oct daily 10–6

MALCÉSINE

Best places to see, ➤ 42–43.

PESCHIERA DEL GARDA

Between Sirmione (➤ 52–53) and Peschiera the visitor crosses from Lombardy to Veneto, making Peschiera the first village of the Riviera of Olives. Because of its position, where the Mincio river leaves the lake, the site of Peschiera has always been important. The Romans had a town here, while under the Lombards a fishing village grew up, and the Scaligeri built a castle and a walled harbour to defend the river crossing. The castle is mentioned by Dante in the *Divine Comedy*. It was destroyed by the Austrians but they reinforced the walls, making the village one of the corners of their 'defensive quadrilateral'. After the Austrians were defeated the walls were not needed, but were too massive to demolish.

West of Peschiera, visitors can see the sites of the two battles of 24 June 1859. On that day, a Piemontian army under Vittorio Emanuele II fought the right wing of the Austrian army close to a village now called San Martino della Battaglia, while a short distance to the south, at Solferino, the French under Napoleon III attacked the main Austrian army under Emperor Franz Josef. More than 40,000 men were killed or wounded, the defeated Austrians being allowed to retreat by the exhausted victors. Today, each of the sites has an ossuary chapel. Below the chapel at Solferino is a museum, and on a hilltop nearby is a monument to the founding of the Red Cross, a result of this battle.

✚ 16S ✉ At the eastern end of Lake Garda's southern shore 🍴 La Torretta (€€), Via G Galilei 12; 045 7550108 🚌 Regular buses from Desenzano

RIVA DEL GARDA

Situated at the northern end of the lake, Riva is northern Garda's most famous holiday resort. The town maintains its character as a fishing/trading port even though the visitors outnumber the locals. The heart of the town is Piazza Tre Novembre, dominated by the Torre Apponale, a 13th-century clocktower, and the arched buildings of the old town hall. A pleasant walk along the shore leads to the **moated castle** built to protect the town from pirates. The castle now houses an excellent museum of local history and an art gallery, and its irresistible approach – over a double-arched bridge and now-fixed drawbridge – ensures a steady stream of

visitors. Among other things, you can see objects from the prehistoric dwellings discovered beside Lake Ledro, the tiny lake to the west of Riva. From the town, you can drive to the top of Monte Brione or take the *funivia* for the short ride to the Bastione for tremendous views of the lake.

✚ 18H ✉ At the northern tip of Lake Garda 🍴 Ristorante alla Torre (€€), Via Mafei 8; 0464 553453 🚌 Regular buses along both lake shores
🛳 Regular lake steamers

Castle/museum

☎ 0464 573869 🕐 Apr–Sep Tue–Sun 10:30–6:30, also Mon Jun–Sep
✋ Inexpensive

SALÒ

Salò is at the farthest reach of an inlet of Lake Garda, an enviable position that shelters it from winds. The town has a fine 15th-century cathedral that houses some excellent artwork, including a polyptych by Paolo Veneziano. Look for the equally attractive 16th-century Palazzo Municipale. On the first floor is a bust of Gasparo Bertolotti (known as Gasparo da Salò), who is usually credited with the invention of the violin.

North of Salò is Gardone Riviera. Here, be sure to visit the **Botanical Gardens,** first planted by Dr Arthur Hruska early in the 20th century and since taken over by the artist André Heller, who has added works combining art and ecology. Also worth visiting is **Il Vittoriale** (Vittoriale degli Italiani), an extraordinary complex constructed by Gabriele d'Annunzio, regarded as one of Italy's most flamboyant characters. He was a poet and soldier, and leader of the disastrous campaign to occupy Fiume (Rijeka) in 1919. In his will d'Annunzio left Il Vittoriale to the State. It is a collection of buildings, many in art nouveau style, and an open-air theatre. D'Annunzio's house is much as he left it and you can also see his mausoleum, which is as extravagant as the man himself.

Beyond Gardone are the twin towns of Toscalano-Maderno, linked by a car ferry to Torri del Benaco, and Gargagno, where the Villa Fetrenelli was the seat of government of Mussolini's ill-fated Salò Republic.

✚ 13N ✉ In a deep bay of Lake Garda's western shore 🍴 Ristorante Lepanto (€€), Lungolargo Zanardelli 67; 0365 20428; www.hotelristorante lepanto.it 🚌 Regular buses from Desenzano 🚢 Regular lake steamers

Giardino Botanico

✉ Via Roma, Gardone Riviera ☎ 0336 410877; www.hellergarden.com
🕐 Mid-Mar to mid-Oct daily 9–7 🚌 Regular buses 🚢 Regular lake steamers ✋ Moderate

Il Vittoriale

✉ Gardone Sopra ☎ 0365 296511 🕐 Park: Apr–Sep daily 8:30–8; Oct–Mar 9–5. House: Apr–Sep Tue–Sun 9:30–7; Oct–Mar 9–1, 2–5. War Museum: Apr–Sep Thu–Tue 9:30–7; Oct–Mar 9–1, 2–5 🚢 Regular lake steamers ✋ Expensive

SIRMIONE

Best places to see, ➤ 52–53.

TIGNALE AND TREMÓSINE

High above Lake Garda's western shore lie two plateaux from where there are wonderful views of the lake. Much of the main road along Garda's western shore is carved through solid rock, tunnelling for long distances through a mountain that drops almost straight into the lake. Far above this, reached by a twisting precipitous road that leaves the main road north of Gargagno, are the Tignale and the Tremósine, separated by the San Michele Valley. The views are spectacular and the 30km (19-mile) road has been called the most beautiful drive in the world. The sanctuary of **Madonna di Montecastello**, at Tignale, is a highlight, filled with art treasures and with an incomparable view. In the village of Pieve, buildings perch over vertical cliffs, and north of it the road drops through a dramatic narrow chasm before rejoining the main shore road. The drive is not for the faint of heart.

✚ 15K/16J 🍴 Miralago (€), Piazza Cozzaglio 2, Tremósine; 0365 953001
🚌 Infrequent buses from the larger lakeside towns

Madonna di Montecastello
✉ Tignale ☎ 0365 73019 🕓 Sun 10–12:30, 5–7

TORBOLE

From a distance Torbole is a great sight with its fjord-like lake, the vast wedges of white rock falling into the water, and the many windsurfers who descend on the town each summer to exploit Garda's dependable winds. Mountain-biking and climbing add to the attractions of sailing and surfing, giving Torbole a young, energetic feel. In Piazza Veneto, a plaque notes that Goethe set out from Torbole on the journey that ended with his arrest at Malcésine, and it was here that he began work on his *Iphigenia*.

✚ 18H ✉ Northern tip of Lake Garda 🚌 Regular buses along both lake shores 🚢 Regular lake steamers

Lake Iseo

Lake Iseo is the fifth-largest of the lakes, 24km (15 miles) long and 5km (3 miles) across at its widest. However, at that widest point the lake is almost filled by Monte Isola, the largest island not only on any of the Italian lakes but on any lake in Europe.

✚ 8D

ISEO

Iseo has a 12th-century church that holds the remains of several members of the Oldofredi family, local lords in medieval times. One tomb is built into the façade. The Oldofredi were also responsible for the castle that is now incorporated into the village hall. The village's lake front offers walks with fine views.

Iseo can be used as a base for exploring the southern part of the lake. To the west is Sarnico, terminus for lake steamers and trains from Bergamo. It is an interesting town with the remains of fortifications, echoes of its past as a fishing port and buildings designed by Sommarciga, one of Italy's foremost art nouveau architects. Between Iseo and Sarnico is Paratico, with a ruined castle, where it's claimed Dante once stayed. Northeastwards from Iseo, the village of Pilzone is pleasantly set behind a headland.

✚ 8D ✉ Southern shore of Lake Iseo 🍴 Il Paiolo (€€), Piazza Mazzini, 9; 030 9821074 🚌 Regular buses from Bréscia 🚢 Regular lake steamers

LÓVERE AND LAKE ISEO'S WESTERN SHORE

Before exploring the western shore take a detour from Pisogne to visit the historically important Val Camonica. On the valley rocks prehistoric humans have engraved and painted a **tribal record** extending from at least 5,000BC until the time of the Romans. Several groups of these rock engravings are open to visit, and the best of the work is in the vicinity of Capo di Ponte, where there is a museum on the engravings, and marked walks around the sites. The Archeodromo at Cenno has a reconstructed tribal village.

On the northern shore, Lóvere is a town of great character and interest, with the remains of medieval fortifications, including three surviving towers, and an art gallery in the beautiful 19th-century Palazzo Tadini. Near Lóvere are the two *bögns* of Castro and Zorzino, huge sheets of limestone that plunge steeply into the lake.

✚ 9D

Parco della Incisioni Rupestiri (National Rock Engravings Park)

✉ Capo di Ponte ☎ Park: 0364 42140. Museum: 0364 42091 🕐 Park: Tue–Sun 8–7:30; closes 4:30 Oct–Apr. Museum: Mon–Fri 9–4 👋 Moderate 🍴 Osteria Moderna & Antica (€–€€), Via Santa Maria 14/a, Lóvere; 035 983382 🚌 Regular bus service from Pisogne

MONTE ISOLA AND LAKE ISEO'S EASTERN SHORE

The eastern lake shore is dominated by Monte Isola, the largest island on any lake in Europe. It is traffic-free, with excellent walking. The island is accessed by boat from Sulzano (from which a long uphill walk leads to the lovely 15th-century church of Santa Maria del Giogo) or from Sala Marasino. Here, the garden of Villa Martinengo includes the remains of a Roman villa among the flower beds. You then take the winding road towards Zone and Europe's finest examples of **erosion pillars** – tall towers of glacial moraine created by uneven erosion. Some pillars are spectacularly high and are topped by huge boulders.

On the eastern shore, the final village is Pisogne, where the church, Santa Maria della Neve, has been called the 'Poor Man's Sistine Chapel' for the quality of the frescoes by Romanino.

✚ 9D

Erosion Pillars

✉ Zone, along a narrow, twisting road from Marone 🍴 Trattoria Cacciatore (€€), Via Molini 28, Sulzano; 030 985184

VERONA

Verona's historic *centro storico* – a UNESCO World Heritage Site – sits inside a curve of the river Adige, and is anchored by the main squares of Piazza Bra and Piazza della Erbe. One side of Piazza Bra is formed by the immense first-century AD Arena. Piazza della Erbe is the scene of the busy daily market. Most of Verona's major sights are within a five-minute walk of these two landmarks, which are connected by the pedestrianized Via Mazzini, Verona's smartest shopping street.

Although it's an out-and-out fraud built in the 1930s, most visitors can't resist stepping into the courtyard of Casa di Guilietta to see the balcony of Shakespeare's entirely fictional heroine, a few steps from Piazza della Erbe. Beyond it is one of the original Roman city gates. Another larger one from the first century, Porta Borsari, spans Corso Porta Borsari near the other end of Piazza della Erbe.

✚ 12F

Arena

The Arena held more than 22,000 people when it was the scene of gladiatorial spectacles in the first century AD, and is today Italy's best-preserved Roman arena. Since 1913, one of Europe's most renowned summer opera festivals, the *Stagione Lyrico di Verona*, has been staged here.

www.arena.it

✉ Piazza Bra ☎ 045 8003204 🕐 Tue–Sun 8:30–7:30, Mon 1:30–7:30; opera days 8:15–3:30 💷 Inexpensive 🍴 Pizzeria Torre 5 (€), Corso Porta Nuova 9 (enter from Via Ghiaia); 045 597832

Castelvecchio and Ponte Scaligero

The combined genius of medieval engineering and the contemporary Venetian architect Carlo Scarpa have created a brilliant art gallery. It sits inside the Scaligeri dynasty's impressive 14th-century castle, beside the Adige. Even if you don't care for the outstanding art collections, it's worth seeing for the castle and its redesign – architects from all over the world visit for inspiration.

Inside are excellent medieval sculptures, masterpieces of Gothic and Renaissance painting, 14th-century jewels and works by contemporary artists. The castellated bridge is for pedestrians.

✉ Corso Castelvecchio (end of Corso Cavour) ☎ 045 594734 ⏰ Tue–Sun 8:30–7:30, Mon 1:30–7:30 🍴 Osteria Casa Vino (€€), Vicolo Morette 8; 045 8004337 ✋ Inexpensive

Duomo di Santa Maria Matricolare

Verona's cathedral is a textbook of Romanesque, Gothic and Renaissance styles, added with each subsequent age. The Romanesque portal surrounded by stone saints dates from the cathedral's beginnings in 1139. Inside, treasures include the 16th-century choir screen by Michele Sanmicheli and Titian's *Assumption*, in the first chapel on the left.

www.cattedralediverona.it

✉ Piazza Duomo ☎ 045 595627 ⏰ Mar–Oct Mon–Sat 10–5:30, Sun 1:30–5:30; Nov–Feb Tue–Sat 10–1, 1:30–5, Sun 1–5 ✋ Inexpensive

Giardini Guisti

Across the river from the historic centre is one of the finest Renaissance gardens in Italy. Planted in the 15th century, the Giusti gardens rise from manicured lawns bordered by hedges and decorated with statues, to a leafy hillside. Paths climb through the trees for downward views that show off the hedge patterns and a garden maze, leading eventually to a balcony at the top in the form of a grotesque carved face.

✉ Via Giardini Giusti 2 ☎ 045 8034029 ⏰ Apr–Sep daily 9–8; Oct–Mar 9–sunset ✋ Inexpensive

Piazza dei Signori

Best places to see, ➤ 46–47.

Sant'Anastasia

Verona's Scala family had a hand in nearly everything in the city. They commissioned this church dedicated to Sant'Anastasia around 1290, and it was built throughout the following century. Highlights include the Pisanello fresco of *St George and the Princess*, and the pair of holy-water fonts just inside the door.

✉ Piazza Sant'Anastasia ☎ 045 592813
🕐 Mar–Oct Mon–Sat 9–6, Sun 1–6; Nov–Feb Tue–Sat 10–1, 1:30–5, Sun 1–5
✋ Inexpensive 🍴 Osteria Sottoriva (€–€€), Via Sottoriva 10; 045 8014323

San Zeno

The church of San Zeno Major is a bit removed from Verona's compact historic centre but it's worth a stroll along the river to reach it. One of the finest remaining examples of Italian Romanesque architecture, the church was built in the early 12th century, although some of the 48 outstanding bronze panels on the front are from the previous century. Be sure to see the freshly restored frescoes and the autographs of early pilgrims on the wall to the right of the altar. Legend holds that the Frankish King Pepin, known to have attended the consecration of the original ninth-century church, is buried under the bell tower.

✉ Piazza San Zeno ☎ 045 8006120 🕐 Mar–Oct Mon–Sat 8:30–6, Sun 1–6; Nov–Feb Tue–Sat 10–1, 1:30–5, Sun 1–5
✋ Inexpensive 🍴 Rosa Blu (€–€€), Piazza Corrubio 29; 045 8036731

Teatro Romano and Museo Archeologico

The Roman theatre built into the steep riverbank above the Roman bridge of Ponte Pietro is now the venue for a summer Shakespeare festival and concerts. Visit in the morning for the best views of old Verona, below. Above the theatre, the former monastery of St Jerome houses a small museum filled with Roman statues, columns, stone carvings, mosaics, bronzes and other items. The small San Girolamo church, part of the museum, has 15th-century frescoes.

✉ Regaste Redentore 2 ☎ 045 0000360 ⏱ Tue–Sun 8:30–7:30, Mon 1:30–7:30 (earlier in winter and performance nights) ✋ Inexpensive

HOTELS

BRÉSCIA AND LAKE ISEO

Master (€€–€€€)

Lovely old palazzo close to the castle. Very comfortable, and with parking on site.

✉ Via Appollonio 72, 25100 Bréscia ☎ 030 399037

Moderno (€€)

Small, very pleasant hotel near the heart of town.

✉ Piazza 13 Martiri 21, 24065 Lóvere ☎ 035 960607

Trattoria Cacciatore (€)

A small B&B on the hillside, with cordial owners and a traditional restaurant. Clean, attractive rooms, with shared bathrooms.

✉ Via Molini 28, Sulzano ☎ 030 985184; www.trattoriacacciatore.it

LAKE GARDA

Caravel (€€€)

Complex of buildings around a swimming pool in a park of palm and olive trees. Terrific views and good restaurant.

✉ Via Tamas 2, 25010 Limone sul Garda ☎ 0365 954040; www.caravelnet.it

Castello (€€)

Right at the lakeside, with a small beach. Good facilities, including a garden, private jetty, bicycle storage area and a Jacuzzi.

✉ Via Paina 3, 37018 Malcésine ☎ 045 7400233; www.h-c.it ⏰ Apr–Oct

Grand Hotel Terme (€€€)

Luxurious spa hotel at the lake edge in the centre of town, with two swimming pools and a garden.

✉ Viale Marconi 7, 25019 Sirmione ☎ 030 916261; www.termedisirmione.com ⏰ Apr–Oct

Nonna Ebe (€)

A small, inexpensive hotel with a good terrace restaurant and reasonable facilities, right in the centre of town.

✉ Via Calsone 9, 25087 Salò ☎ 0365 43639

Sirmione (€€–€€€)

A good hotel for a romantic break. At the boat jetty, with its own spa and restaurant. Some rooms have terraces with lake views.

✉ Piazza Castello 19, 25019 Sirmione ☎ 030 916331; www.termedisirmione.com 🕔 Mar–Nov

Villa Capri (€€)

Glorious position. The lakeside garden offers shady trees and sunloungers around a pool. Most rooms have balconies.

✉ Via Zanardelli 172, 25083 Gardone Riviera ☎ 0365 21537; www.hotelvillacapri.com 🕔 Apr–Oct

Villa Nicolli (€€)

Surrounded by a large, lush garden, the hotel has a pool and a good restaurant. Most rooms have balconies.

✉ Via Cattoni 5, 38066 Riva del Garda ☎ 0464 552589; www.hotelvillanicolli.com 🕔 Mid-Mar to Oct

Vittorio (€€)

This hotel can't be beaten on location as it's right at the edge of the old harbour, making for pleasant views. No restaurant, but easy access to some of the best in town.

✉ Via Porto Vecchio 4, 25015 Desenzano del Garda ☎ 030 9912245, www.gardalake.it/hotelvittorio 🕔 Mar–Nov

VERONA

Accademia (€€)

On Verona's smart pedestrianized shopping street, the Accademia offers all the mod-cons, in classically decorated rooms. The restaurant serves local dishes, in an elegant setting.

✉ Via Scala 10, 37121 Verona ☎ 045 596222; www.accademiavr.it

Due Torri Baglioni (€€€)

The best in town, near Piazza della Erbe and the Arena. This five-star hotel has elegant rooms and personal service.

✉ Piazza Sant'Anastasia 4, 37121 Verona ☎ 045 595044; www.baglionihotels.com

RESTAURANTS

LAKE ISEO

Al Desco (€€)

Superb fish restaurant – but also with good pasta dishes – in a lovely setting. Excellent value.

✉ Piazza XX Septembre 19, Sarnico ☎ 035 910740; www.ristorantealdesco.it 🕐 Daily lunch and dinner

Osteria Moderno & Antico (€–€€)

Risottino amalgamato al pesce persico (a rice-and-fish dish) is not uncommon on menus around the lakes, but the version at this restaurant is uncommonly tasty.

✉ Via Santa Maria 14/a, Lóvere ☎ 035 983382 🕐 Thu–Tue lunch and dinner

Il Paiolo (€€)

The best on this section of the lake. A varied menu with something for everyone. Very good desserts.

✉ Piazza Mazzini 9, Iseo ☎ 030 9821074 🕐 Thu–Tue lunch and dinner

Trattoria al Porto (€€)

This historic restaurant made its name baking the local white lake fish *(tinca)* in a traditional but unusual way; to see why it made them famous, order the *tinca al forno con polenta*.

✉ Porto del Pescatori 12, Clusane ☎ 030 989014; www.alportoclusane.it 🕐 Thu–Tue lunch and dinner

Trattoria Cacciatore (€–€€)

Enjoy hearty traditional dishes, along with views over the town and lake to Monte Isola.

✉ Via Molini 28, Sulzano ☎ 030 985184; www.trattoriacacciatore.it 🕐 Wed–Sun lunch and dinner, Mon lunch

BRÉSCIA

Gambero Rosso (€€)

This chic city restaurant offers white linens, fresh flowers, Amarone as the house wine and meat prepared just as ordered, and at moderate prices. Order the *casconcelli* (local ravioli), veal or any red meat dish with confidence.

✉ Via Laura Cereto 8A ☎ 030 43338 ◔ Wed–Fri, Sun, Mon lunch, dinner, Sat dinner

La Sosta (€€€)

Housed in a beautiful, elegant 17th-century building, which complements the fine food.

✉ Via San Martino della Battaglia 20 ☎ 030 295603 ◔ Tue–Sat lunch and dinner

LAKE GARDA

Le Ancore della Bastia (€€)

Seafood lovers who are tired of dining on lake fish will find shellfish and saltwater fish here, served in tasty paella, with pasta or delicately grilled.

✉ Via Bastia, Lazise ☎ 045 6470779, www.leancoredellabastia.it ◔ Daily lunch and dinner

Antica Trattoria alle Rose (€€)

Delightful building and decor, good menu, fine food and service. Although the lake fish is always freshly caught and delicious, the restaurant is known for its lamb and kid from Tremósine and the Val Sabbia, often prepared with local wild mushrooms.

✉ Via Costalungo 18, Salò ☎ 0365 43220 ◔ Thu–Tue lunch and dinner

Caffé Italia (€)

A small, but very pleasant restaurant and wine bar close to the old port. Good food and excellent service.

✉ Piazza Malvezzi 19, Desenzano del Garda ☎ 030 9141243; www.ristorantecaffeitalia.it ◔ Tue–Sun lunch and dinner

Esplanade (€€€)

Absolutely first class. Speciality pastas and such mouth-watering dishes as mountain lamb in herbs. Highly recommended.

✉ Via Lario 10, Desenzano del Garda ☎ 030 9143361; www.ristorante-esplanade.com ◔ Lunch and dinner

Il Gallo Rosso (€)

Excellent restaurant that offers a special 'drink-included' price. The cheese-filled ravioli are especially good, as are the tortellini.

✉ Vicolo Tomacelli 4, Salò ☎ 0365 520757 🕓 Thu–Sun lunch and dinner

Il Giardino delle Esperidi (€€)

Beautiful garden restaurant with menu and food to match. Revel in local specialities, with an antipasto of shaved Parmesan and truffles from Monte Baldo, followed by duck in Amarone wine from nearby Valpolicella.

✉ Via Mameli 1, Bardolino ☎ 045 6210477 🕓 Thu–Tue dinner

Ristorante Lepanto (€€)

Tortellini bursting with roasted pumpkin, lake fish perfumed with thyme and rosemary and roasted in salt, young beef with creamy porcini mushroom sauce – the food here is special.

✉ Lungolago Zanardelli 67, Salò ☎ 0365 20428; www.hotelristorantelepanto.it 🕓 Thu–Tue lunch and dinner

Ristorante alla Torre (€–€€)

Serves regional dishes such as *risotto porcini* and grilled *lavarello*, a local lake fish.

✚ Via Mafei 8, Riva del Garda ☎ 046 4553453 🕓 Daily lunch and dinner

La Tortuga (€€€)

One of the best places on Garda's western shore. Specialities include lake fish and a secret fettuccine recipe. Dinner reservations are advisable, but tables are usually available at lunchtime.

✉ Via XXIV Maggio 5, Gargnano ☎ 0365 71251 🕓 Wed–Mon lunch, dinner

Trattoria Vecchia Malcésine (€€€)

Fine dining with a cozy ambiance. Indulge your palate with the *Trilogia di Lago e Frutta:* three types of lake fish, each prepared differently, with ingredients as diverse as banana, olives, mango, coffee and curry. Reservations are suggested.

✉ Via Pisort 6, Malcésine ☎ 045 7400469; www.vecchiamalcesine.com 🕓 Lunch and dinner

VERONA
Accademia (€€)
Midway between the Arena and Scaligeri Tombs. Very good menu.
Try Treviso-style ravioli with smoked ricotta.
✉ Via Scala 10 ☎ 045 8006072; www.ristoranteaccademia.com ⏰ Jun, Jul
daily lunch and dinner; Sep–May Mon–Sat lunch and dinner

Antica Bottega del Vino (€€)
Along a side street off Via Mazzini. Atmospheric, with bottle-lined
walls. Try the chef's tortellini or the polenta dishes.
✉ Via Scudo di Francia 3 ☎ 045 8004535; www.bottegavini.it ⏰ Lunch and
dinner. Closed Tue except during opera season

Osteria Casa Vino (€€)
Specializing in meat dishes, such as the signature rabbit
cacciatore, in a homey, historic setting.
✉ Vicolo Morette 8 ☎ 045 8004337 ⏰ Wed–Mon lunch and dinner

ENTERTAINMENT

CLASSICAL MUSIC
Arena di Verona
Site of the summer opera festival, from late June through August.
✉ Piazza Bra 28, Verona. Box office Via Dietro Anfiteatro 6b ☎ 045
8051811. Box office 045 8005151; www.arena.it

CLUBS
Alter Ego Club
Dance on the terrace while looking out across the city.
✉ Via Torricelle 9, Verona ☎ 045 915130 ⏰ Fri, Sat 11:30pm–4am

Kursaal
An eclectic mix of music, from current hits to ballroom classics.
✉ Via San Martino della Battaglia, Sirmione ☎ 030 919163

Rivabar
Music and cocktails in a lively contemporary setting.
✉ Largo Medaglie d'Oro, Riva del Garda ☎ 0464 551969; www.rivabar.it

Index

Acknowledgements

The Automobile Association would like to thank the following photographers, companies and picture libraries for their assistance in the preparation of this book.

Abbreviations for the picture credits are as follows – (t) top; (b) bottom; (c) centre; (l) left; (r) right; (AA) AA World Travel Library.

4l Villa Balbianello, Lago di Como, AA/A Mockford & N Bonetti; **4c** road along Lago di Garda, AA/A Mockford & N Bonetti; **4r** Scaligeri Castle, Sirmione, AA/A Mockford & N Bonetti; **5l** Malcésine, AA/M Jourdan; **5r** Bellágio, AA/A Mockford & N Bonetti; **6/7** Villa Balbianello, Lago di Como, AA/A Mockford & N Bonetti; **8/9** Malcésine, AA/A Mockford & N Bonetti; **10/11t** Sirmione, AA/M Jourdan; **10c** Ferry, AA/A Mockford & N Bonetti; **10/11b** Lago di Lugano, AA/A Mockford & N Bonetti; **11c** Villa Carlotta, AA/A Mockford & N Bonetti; **12b** aubergines, AA/D Miterdiri; **12/13t** squashes, AA/M Jourdan; **12/13b** porcini mushrooms, AA/M Jourdan; **13t** pasta, AA/M Jourdan; **14bl** Limoncello, AA/M Jourdan; **14/15t** ice cream, AA/M Jourdan; **14br** wine detail, AA/A Mockford & N Bonetti; **15bl** cheese, AA/A Mockford & N Bonetti; **16** Lago di Garda, AA/A Mockford & N Bonetti; **17** Salò, AA/A Mockford & N Bonetti; **18/19t** Bardolino, AA/A Mockford & N Bonetti; **18/19b** ice cream cones, AA/A Mockford & N Bonetti; **19br** Ballino, AA/A Mockford & N Bonetti; **20/21** road along Lago di Garda, AA/A Mockford & N Bonetti; **28bl** Carnival, AA/D Miterdiri; **28bl** ferry times, AA/A Mockford & N Bonetti; **31bl** sign, AA/T Harris; **34/35** Scaligeri Castle, Sirmione, AA/A Mockford & N Bonetti; **36/37** Bellágio, AA/M Jourdan; **37br** Bellágio, AA/M Jourdan; **38/39** Duomo, Milan, AA/M Jourdan; **39tl** Piazza Duomo, Milan, AA/M Jourdan; **40tl** Isola Bella, AA/M Jourdan; **40/41** gardens, Isola Bella, AA/M Jourdan; **41br** Isola Bella, AA/C Sawyer; **42/43t** Harbourside cafés, Malcésine, AA/A Mockford & N Bonetti; **42/43b** Malcésine, AA/A Mockford & N Bonetti; **44tl** balcony, Isola San Giúlio, AA/M Jourdan; **44/45** Orto San Giúlio, AA/M Jourdan; **46** Loggia del Consiglio, Verona, AA/A Mockford & N Bonetti; **46/47** Scaligeri Tombs, Verona, AA/A Mockford & N Bonetti; **48bl** Contarini fountain, Bergamo, AA/M Jourdan; **48/49** Piazza Vecchia, Bergamo, AA/A Souter; **50/51** Santa Caterina del Sasso, AA/P Bennett; **52** Castle, Sirmione, AA/A Mockford & N Bonetti; **53** Roman Villa ruins, Sirmione, AA/A Mockford & N Bonetti; **54** Gardens of Villa Carlotta, Tremezzo, AA/A Mockford & N Bonetti; **55** Cupid and Psyche, Villa Carlotta, Tremezzo, AA/A Mockford & N Bonetti; **56/57** Malcésine, AA/M Jourdan; **58** Salò, AA/A Mockford & N Bonetti; **60** child at zoo, AA/E Davies; **62** Lugano, AA/A Mockford & N Bonetti; **63tr** chalet, AA/A Mockford & N Bonetti; **65tl** rock climber, Lago di Gardo, AA/A Mockford & N Bonetti; **66/67** Bellágio, AA/C Sawyer; **68/69** view of Lago Gardo, AA/A Mockford & N Bonetti; **69** view to Prabione, AA/A Mockford & N Bonetti; **70/71** Bellágio, AA/A Mockford & N Bonetti; **73b** La Scala, AA/C Sawyer; **75** Castello Storzesco, AA/M Jourdan; **76** Museo Nazionale della Scienza e della Tecnologia, AA/M Jourdan; **77** Brera Art Gallery, AA/M Jourdan; **78/79** Santa Maria della Grazie, AA/C Sawyer; **80/81** Galleria Vittorio Emanuele, AA/C Sawyer; **83tr** Palazzo della Ragione, AA/M Jourdan; **91** Lago di Varese, AA/A Mockford & N Bonetti; **92/93** casino, Campione d'Italia, ©saturno dona'/Alamy; **94/95** Morcote, Marka ©Michele Bella; **96/97** Lugano, AA/A Mockford & N Bonetti; **98** Swissminiatur, AA/A Baker; **100/101** Angera, AA/A Mockford & N Bonetti; **102** Arona, AA/A Mockford & N Bonetti; **104/105** Isola dei Pescatori, AA/C Sawyer; **100/107** Castelli di Cannero, AA/A Mockford & N Bonetti; **107** Cannobio, AA/P Bennett; **108/109** Laveno, AA/P Bennett; **110** Villa Taranto, Pallanza, AA/P Bennett; **110/111** Pallanza, AA/A Mockford & N Bonetti; **112/113** Lago Maggiore, AA/A Mockford & N Bonetti; **113** Isola Bella, AA/A Mockford & N Bonetti; **114/115** Madonna del Sasso, AA/A Baker; **116/117** Basilica of San Giúlio, Isola San Giúlio, AA/M Jourdan; **118/119** Omegna, Marka ©Walter Zerla; **120/121** Varese, AA/M Jourdan; **129** Menaggio, AA/A Mockford & N Bonetti; **131** Bellan Abbey, AA/M Jourdan; **132/133** Cadenabbia, AA/M Jourdan; **134/135** Duomo, Como Town, AA/M Jourdan; **137** Basilica di San Fedele, Como Town, AA/M Jourdan; **138/139** Gravedona, APT del Conasco; **140/141** Piazza Cermenati, Lecco, AA/M Jourdan; **141** Sala Comacina, AA/A Mockford & N Bonetti; **142/143** Menággio, AA/A Mockford & N Bonetti; **144/145** Varenna, AA/M Jourdan; **146/147** Villa Balbianello, Lenno, AA/A Mockford & N Bonetti; **148/149** Colleoni Chapel, Bergamo, AA/M Jourdan; **150/151** San Pellegrino Terme, AA/P Bennett; **157** Lago d'Idro, AA/A Mockford & N Bonetti; **158/159** The Broletto and Torre del Popolo, AA/A Mockford & N Bonetti; **160/161** Museo della Citta, Brescia, AA/A Mockford & N Bonetti; **162/163** boat, Desenzano, AA/M Jourdan; **164** Lago di Garda, AA/A Mockford & N Bonetti; **165** Scaligeri Castle, Lazise, AA/A Mockford & N Bonetti; **166/167** Limone sul Garda, AA/M Jourdan; **168** Riva del Gard, AA/M Jourdan; **169** Duomo, Salò; **170** Salò, AA/A Mockford & N Bonetti; **172** Lago d'Iseo, AA/M Jourdan; **173** Lóvere, AA/P Bennett; **174/175** Monte Isola, AA/M Jourdan; **175** Verona, AA/A Mockford & N Bonetti; **176** Castle, Verona, AA/A Mockford & N Bonetti; **177** Giardino Guisti, Verona, AA/A Mockford & N Bonetti; **178** Chiesa San Anastasia, Verona, AA/A Mockford & N Bonetti; **178/179** Amphitheatre, Verona, AA/C Sawyer

Every effort has been made to trace the copyright holders, and we apologise in advance for any accidental errors. We would be happy to apply the corrections in the following edition of this publication.

Sight locator index

This index relates to the maps on the covers. We have given map references to the main sights of interest in the book. Grid references in italics indicate sights featured on town plans. Some sights within towns may not be plotted on the maps.

Dear Reader

Your comments, opinions and recommendations are very important to us. Please help us to improve our travel guides by taking a few minutes to complete this simple questionnaire.

You do not need a stamp (unless posted outside the UK). If you do not want to cut this page from your guide, then photocopy it or write your answers on a plain sheet of paper.

Send to: **The Editor, AA World Travel Guides,**
FREEPOST SCE 4598, Basingstoke RG21 4GY.

Your recommendations...

We always encourage readers' recommendations for restaurants, nightlife or shopping — if your recommendation is used in the next edition of the guide, we will send you a **FREE AA Guide** of your choice from this series. Please state below the establishment name, location and your reasons for recommending it.

_____

_____

_____

_____

_____

_____

Please send me **AA Guide** _____

About this guide...

Which title did you buy?

AA _____

Where did you buy it? _____

When? m m / y y

Why did you choose this guide? _____

_____

_____

_____

_____

Did this guide meet your expectations?

Exceeded ☐   Met all ☐   Met most ☐   Fell below ☐

Were there any aspects of this guide that you particularly liked? _____

_____

_____

_____

continued on next page...

Is there anything we could have done better? _____
_____
_____
_____

About you...
Name (*Mr/Mrs/Ms*) _____
Address _____
_____
_____ Postcode _____

Daytime tel nos _____
Email _____

Please only give us your mobile phone number or email if you wish to hear from us about other products and services from the AA and partners by text or mms, or email.

Which age group are you in?
Under 25 ☐   25–34 ☐   35–44 ☐   45–54 ☐   55–64 ☐   65+ ☐

How many trips do you make a year?
Less than one ☐   One ☐   Two ☐   Three or more ☐

Are you an AA member? Yes ☐   No ☐

About your trip...
When did you book? m m / y y   When did you travel? m m / y y

How long did you stay? _____

Was it for business or leisure? _____

Did you buy any other travel guides for your trip? _____

If yes, which ones? _____
_____
_____

Thank you for taking the time to complete this questionnaire. Please send it to us as soon as possible, and remember, you do not need a stamp (*unless posted outside the UK*).

AA Travel Insurance call 0800 072 4168 or visit www.theAA.com